Science for Primary Teachers

An Audit and Self-Study Guide

Graham Peacock

EDUCATIONAL

Aldine Place
London
W12 8AW

Tel: 0181-740 2268
Fax: 0181-743 8451
e-mail: he@lettsed.co.uk

A CIP catalogue record is available from the British Library

ISBN 1-85805-350-1
Copyright Graham Peacock © 1998
Reprinted 1998

Designed and edited by Topics – The Creative Partnership, Exeter
Illustrations by Neil Annat

Printed and bound in Great Britain by Progressive Printing (UK) Ltd, Leigh-on-Sea, Essex

Contents

The Letts QTS Series offers support for all those preparing to become teachers and working towards Qualified Teacher Status (QTS). The content, teaching approaches and practical ideas are useful for trainee teachers, teacher tutors and mentors, and teacher educators in higher education.

The Letts QTS Series addresses the new standards for QTS and the content of the Initial Teacher Training National Curriculum (ITTNC). These are central to the improvement of standards in schools. The series is specifically designed to help all trainee teachers cover the content of the ITTNC and achieve the national standards in order to be awarded QTS.

The short series handbook *QTS: A Practical Introduction* gives trainees an overview of the QTS requirements and a more detailed interpretation of each standard.

The other books in the Letts QTS Series offer trainees the chance to audit their knowledge of the content of the subjects in the ITTNC, pinpoint areas of further work, and use support materials to develop their knowledge.

With the exception of information and communications technology, which is covered in a single, integrated volume, books in the Letts QTS Series address separately the needs of trainees preparing to teach in the primary or the secondary phase of schooling. For each type of trainee there are two books per subject:

Book 1 addresses trainees' subject knowledge at their own level by offering a systematic and comprehensive guide to the subject knowledge requirements of the ITTNC. Trainees can check their own knowledge of the subject against that specified in the ITTNC. Section one provides a comprehensive **audit** of this subject knowledge and understanding, with helpful **feedback** and follow-up set out in section two. Having identified areas of subject knowledge for attention, and pinpointed some of the subject's **key ideas**, trainees can then use the materials to map out their **personal learning plan**.

Book 2 for each subject is a handbook of **lesson plans**, **knowledge** and **methods**. This provides details of carefully selected lessons which illustrate effective teaching.

It shows how lesson planning and classroom teaching draw on a high level of subject knowledge. It demonstrates how carefully integrated whole-class teaching and group and individual work can be designed to ensure that pupils make progress in their learning.

There is also a tutor-support pack for each subject.

The Letts QTS Series aims to break down the requirements of QTS into manageable units so that trainees can evaluate and improve their knowledge of each subject. The books in the series are written in a straightforward way by authors who are all experienced teachers, teacher educators, researchers, writers and specialists in their subject areas.

Titles in the Letts QTS Series for primary phase trainees cover English, mathematics and science. Further titles will follow in these subjects for trainees preparing to teach in the secondary phase of schooling. The cross-phase book on information and communications technology is in preparation.

This book contains an *Audit*, which consists of a series of questions about science. The questions are answered in a *Feedback* section which has an identical numbering system. The *Audit* should not be seen as a test given to you by someone else. Rather you should regard it is one of the ways in which you will carry out self-assessment of your developing knowledge and skills in science. This book aims for comprehensive coverage of the science set out in the Initial Teacher Training National Curriculum (ITTNC) for science published by the TTA in May 1998. The sections closely follow the ITTNC for primary students so you can map your knowledge against the standards for qualified teacher status (QTS).

You can **audit** your knowledge before starting work on any area of science. This will help you **revise** and **check** your **knowledge** of that area of science. It will

help you to identify the science you already understand as well as the science you need to know. If you want a very quick indication of your knowledge level you could try to complete the **revision** procedure at the end of some sections of the *Audit*. These revision procedures are repeated, with answers, at the end of matching sections of *Feedback* as a **summary**.

Your tutor may help you by pointing out sections of this book to work through before the relevant part of your taught course. Make notes of all the areas which you feel you need to work on and draw up a **personal learning plan** for each section. There are materials at the end of this book to help you with this. In your personal learning plan you should list the specific questions that you want answering as well as your general areas of uncertainty. Near the end of your course you will need to demonstrate that you have achieved at

least the minimum standards of science knowledge required for QTS. Use the notes you have made in your primary science file as part of the evidence that you have achieved QTS standard in science.

Remember to return to your personal learning plan to keep track of what you have covered. This may help you to assess your own knowledge and highlight those areas you need to work on. Every working day as a teacher you will be assessing pupils and deciding what they should learn next; you will have to start this process with your own knowledge.

You might find it helpful to write short bullet points in response to the audit using one colour. Use a different colour to add points that emerge when you check the feedback. This makes audit fairly quick and graphically shows which areas you are sure of or need work on.

Audit

Early theories of disease

Food preservation

Flat Earth

The creation of the universe

Predicting the future

Disease genes

The environment

Immunization risks

1.1 How science works

(a) Before the discovery of germs how did people account for plagues and diseases?

(b) Pasteur heated food material and sealed it up. He found that heated and sealed food did not decay. What did his experiments suggest about where the agents of decay come from?

Louis Pasteur's name lives on in the word 'pasteurization'.

1.2 Evidence informs and shapes theory

(a) In medieval Europe people thought that bleeding with leeches cured many ills. What questions would you have asked a medieval doctor before agreeing to be bled?

(b) What evidence do you think persuaded people in medieval Europe that the Earth was flat?

(c) What later evidence has changed this view? In other words, how do you know the Earth is a sphere?

Medical procedures are still dictated by fashion. Thirty years ago many children had their tonsils unnecessarily removed.

1.3 Science cannot explain everything

(a) Why can there never be evidence to suggest what came before the creation of the universe?

(b) Why can't science accurately predict the weather next month?

(c) Will science ever be able to predict from genetics which individuals are likely to be violent criminals?

The 'Big Bang'

1.4 Ethical considerations

(a) Why are many people concerned that the identification of the genes that can cause breast cancer, for example, poses moral questions?

(b) After analysis of your genes, would you want to be told if you had a high chance of developing a debilitating disease in your middle age? Explain your thinking.

The amount of genetic knowledge about people is increasing.

(c) The question of disposal of materials at sea is highly contentious. Describe some of the pros and cons of disposing of redundant oil platforms at sea and on land.

Disposal on land is also hazardous.

(d) Should medical researchers tell parents that there is a very slight risk from immunization injections for measles, mumps and rubella?

2 Scientific investigations

Deciding on questions
which will make good
practical investigations

2.1 Not all questions can be investigated practically
(a) Which of these questions could children investigate practically in the primary classroom? Make a brief note about how each one could be investigated.

How far do cars roll off a ramp?
Why do I like chocolate ice cream?
Do most people prefer chocolate ice cream to vanilla?
How fast does sound travel?
How fast does electricity travel?
What will the weather be like tomorrow?
Do you get food poisoning if you eat raw chicken?

Which present practical problems, and what are these?

2.2 Constructing questions which can be investigated
(a) Devise some questions which could be answered practically concerning the best ways to grow bean sprouts for Chinese cookery.

Bean sprouts from the Chinese store probably taste better.

(b) What are the dependent variables in your bean sprout experiments?

(c) The children in your class are interested in the birds which land on the school playground after break. Suggest five questions which might be worth investigating.

Think up some which involve counting.

(d) Distinguish between these words:
• guess • predict • hypothesize

(e) Complete these sentences using the words above.

I _____ that the weight will fall faster than the ball because the weight is heavier than the ball and I think that all heavy things fall faster than lighter ones.

I _____ that the weight will fall faster than the ball, but I've never thought about it before.

I _____ that the weight will fall faster than the ball, based on what I've seen before.

I _____ that the red car will travel faster than the blue one because its wheels are smoother and I think smooth wheels cut down friction.

I _____ that the red car will go faster than the blue one.

I _____ that the blue car will beat the red because it did last time.

(f) Write your own sentences with these words missing and ask a colleague to complete them.

2.3 Planning investigations and controlling variables
If you wanted to investigate in the primary classroom which out of bubble wrap, foam rubber and cloth was the best insulator:

Computers have made measuring less tedious.

(a) What equipment would you need? (Specify fairly precisely.)

Listing variables

(b) What variables would you need to take into account?

(c) What would you measure?

Reliability

(d) How could you ensure that the results were reliable? What do scientists mean by 'reliable'?

Graphing results

(e) How would you present your results? Sketch out your idea. Think about how the appropriate use of colour could enhance your presentation.

> Sketching a graph is a useful way to check that it will work.

2.4 Selecting samples and interpreting data

Measuring the heights in a class

(a) A class measured the heights of boys and girls. They noted that, on average, the girls were taller. Does the data provide evidence to support the following claims? Explain your logic.

> Logic and accuracy are important in interpretation.

Girls are taller than boys.
On average girls are taller than boys.
Jane is taller than Jim. (Both are in the class.)
In this class, on average, girls are taller than boys.
Girls are taller than boys because they mature earlier.
Most girls are taller than most boys.

Sampling bird visits

(b) A class counted the visits made by birds to the school playground after break one day. This is the data they collected:

blackbird	12 visits
sparrow	23 visits
wren	2 visits
pigeon	33 visits

What can the children say about this data which is strictly correct?

2.5 The reasons for anomalous results

Scattergram showing the distance travelled by plasticine weights thrown using a model Roman catapult

> Ancient catapults called 'mangonels' make an excellent introduction to elastic energy.

Scattergram

Anomalous results

(a) Look at the graph above. Which is the anomalous result?

(b) Give some likely causes of this anomalous result.

(c) If you were the teacher of the very bright children who produced this graph what teaching points would you make?

2.6 Interpreting outcomes in the light of scientific evidence

You find that if a circuit contains a length of pencil lead any bulb in the circuit will glow very dimly. If you use a longer piece of pencil lead the bulb glows even more dimly.

A pencil lead resistor dims a bulb.

See section 9.4, Resistance.

(a) What knowledge might you need before you can make sense of these observations?

Making sense of observations

(b) What new knowledge might you have acquired from these observations?

(c) What practical device used in some living rooms is based on this idea?

2.7 Collecting evidence

Ecological investigation

(a) What techniques would you use to collect evidence about changes in the vegetation growing under and near a tree as you move away from its trunk?

Measuring very tall objects

(b) Describe two methods you might use to measure the height of a tall tree.

Application of mathematical information

(c) If you carried out successive tests of a person's reaction time, would you expect every test to give the same result?

Bar charts

(d) If you measured the height of the children in a class what sort of pattern would you expect a bar chart to show? What words would you use in your analysis of the bar chart?

Patterns like this show a normal distribution. (You will see these when assessing pupils).

Line graphs

(e) Draw a quick sketch line graph showing the data below. Make sure you put the values on the correct axes of the graph.

Time	Outside temperature	Time	Outside temperature
9am	10°C	1pm	22°C
10am	12°C	2pm	18°C
11am	18°C	3pm	17°C
12noon	23°C	4pm	19°C

(f) Interpret this data (draw at least four possible pieces of information from the data).

(g) Which is the dependent variable and which is the independent variable?

Continuous variables

(h) Both time and temperature are continuous variables. What other continuous variables can you think of?

Statistics

(i) Check your understanding of statistics and the methods that are used to present them in graph form. The *Further reading* on page 105 suggests books to help you with this.

2.8 Measuring and validity

Valid and reliable

(a) Distinguish between the following words in the context of experimental work:

- reproducibility   • validity   • reliability

Words like this are used in public debate about data concerning health issues such as smoking.

(b) Which of the factors described above is the issue in these problems:

The scientist found that no one else got the same results when they tried her experiment.

The scientist found that his experiment gave different results every time he tried it.

No one trusted the results because the experiment did not control variables.

The teacher gave the children different maths tests and then tried to rank the children in order of ability.

The class teachers got one result when administering the spelling test but the head got another.

Accurate measurement

(c) What factors would you take into account when measuring 20 ml of a liquid?

Parallax error

(d) What is parallax error? How does it affect the accuracy of readings on thermometers?

2.9 Units of measurement

SI (Système Internationale) units are used throughout the world by scientists.

N	J	A	Ω	ml
kg	W	V	°C	dB

These units are considered in more detail in later sections of this book.

(a) What unit of measurement does each abbreviation stand for?

(b) What does each unit measure?

(c) What measuring instrument would you use in each case?

2.10 Graphs and charts

Growth chart

(a) When measuring the growth of a seedling this table was used.

Day	1	2	3	4	5
Height (cm)	3	3	4	5	5

Independent and dependent variables

Which of these two values is the independent variable and which is the dependent variable?

Whilst you do not need to mention these terms with children, you need to know how to handle the different categories of data.

x and y graph axes

(b) When drawing a chart from these values, which is placed on the horizontal (x) axis and which goes on the vertical (y) axis?

(c) What is the difference between a bar chart and a histogram?

Line graph opportunities

(d) In which of these investigations could you use a line graph to show the results:

the number of swings made by a pendulum each minute
the distance a ball is thrown by different people
the colour of eyes of pupils in the class

(e) Draw a sketch scattergram of this information.

Scattergram

Height (cm)	Span of hand (cm)	Height (cm)	Span of hand (cm)
140	15	155	16
185	20	160	18

This simple list could be entered on a computer spreadsheet.

Opportunities for scattergrams

(f) Suggest other investigations which would give information on which to base a scattergram.

(g) Suggest some investigations which would yield information suitable for presentation as a line graph.

2.11 Keys

Vertebrates

(a) Construct a key which children could use to sort vertebrate animals into groups.

See section 6.1, The classification of organisms.

Binary or dichotomous keys

(b) Construct a key which will sort:
- moss
- sycamore tree
- grass
- fern
- rose

One of your questions should ask if it is a flowering plant.

See section 4.9, Flowers.

Leaf key

(c) Use this multiple choice key to identify these leaves.

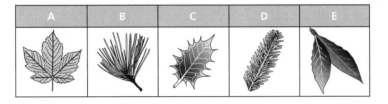

1 If your leaf is glossy   go to Q2
   If your leaf is needle shaped   go to Q3
   If your leaf is not like these go to Q4

2 If your leaf is prickly   it may be holly
   If your leaf is not prickly   it may be laurel

3 If your needle is in a pair   it may be pine
   If your needle is single   it may be fir

4 If your leaf has five points   it may be sycamore
   If your leaf is not like this   go to Q5 ... and so on ...

Construct your own key.

(d) Construct a key of your own written in a similar style. You might choose to make a key about coins, fellow teachers or students. Show it to a colleague to test whether other people can follow it too.

Branch is a key-making program on computers.

Use a published key.

(e) Find a key to follow from an identification book about flowers, trees or insects. Write down the names of books with keys which you have found easy to use. Find *The Clue Book of Flowers* (Allen, G. and Denslow, J., Oxford University Press, 1997) or another title in *The Clue Book* series.

Most identification books have keys; those intended for children avoid technical language.

Key ideas summary
This revision procedure can be done as a quick check at any time.

When conducting investigations scientists need to know ways to control and _____ variables. The _____ variable is the one which we change systematically. The _____ variable is the value which changes in response to changes in the _____ variable. Continuous variables include values such as _____, _____ and _____. On the other hand values like number of bricks or number of insulation layers are examples of _____ variables.

Scientific investigations do not always yield expected or consistent results. This may be because of poor design, incorrect _____ or simply because there was no pattern there to discover. We should also look back at the _____ question when trying to interpret the results of any investigation.

3 Health and safety requirements

3.1 Health, safety and the Law

Asthma problems

(a) Which of these would you not keep in a classroom used by a child with severe asthma?
- small lizard   • guinea pig

(b) Which mammal is suitable for classroom captivity?

Legal constraints

(c) Why could you not keep a grass snake, newt or a frog in your classroom?

> Rare and endangered creatures are protected by law.

(d) Why would you not keep terrapins in the classroom?

3.2 Burning

Safety with candles

(a) What basic precautions would you take when burning candles in the infant classroom?

> Candles are an indispensable part of primary science.

(b) What basic precautions would you take when burning candles in the upper junior classroom?

Burning fabrics

(c) When doing burning tests on fabrics what precautions would you take?

(d) Where can you find information about safety in primary science?

> Local authorities should be able to give guidance on safety.

Safety at the seaside

(e) When investigating rock pools on a rocky seashore what safety precautions would you take?

(f) Every school has an accident book. What sort of accidents should you catalogue in it?

4 Functions of organisms

4.1 All living things show seven life processes

Life processes

Scientists looking for life on other planets will be faced with the problem of defining what it means to be alive. When the Voyager probe went to Mars in 1997 one of the experiments on board was designed to see if anything on the surface of Mars was alive. The scientists used a checklist of the seven life processes.

> How could a visitor to our planet tell that a tree is alive but a car is not?

<table>
<tr><td>

Plant life processes

</td><td>

(a) List the life processes and give an example of each one.

(b) Which of these life processes do you think children find it difficult to associate with plants?

</td><td>

Even things which are definitely alive can appear to be missing life signs.

</td></tr>
</table>

(a) List the life processes and give an example of each one.

Plant life processes

(b) Which of these life processes do you think children find it difficult to associate with plants?

Even things which are definitely alive can appear to be missing life signs.

Is it alive?

(c) Are seeds and cut flowers alive?

Is fire alive?

(d) It is a common misconception among children that fire is alive. What characteristics of fires suggest that they are alive? How would you convince a child that fires are not alive?

4.2 Life processes in humans

Human life processes

(a) How do you know that you are alive?

Is death inevitable if the heart stops beating?

Coma

(b) How can we tell that a person in a coma is alive?

Death

(c) When do doctors finally decide that a person is dead?

4.3 The specialized functions of the human gut

Human gut

(a) Put these major parts of the alimentary canal into the correct order.
  - oesophagus
  - small intestine
  - stomach
  - mouth
  - anus
  - large intestine

The human gut is a long tube where food is broken down. The food value is extracted and absorbed into the blood.

Functions of parts of the gut

(b) Draw a quick labelled sketch of the alimentary canal.

(c) Where do these functions take place?

removal of the water from food waste
absorption of soluble food into the blood
mixing of food with strong acid
chopping of food into small pieces
carrying the food into the stomach.

Each part of the gut does a different job in digestion.

4.4 Human circulation

The function of the heart

(a) Draw a stylized diagram of the heart with its four chambers. Indicate the flow of blood through its two inputs and two outputs.

Blood is pumped under pressure. Each time the heart pumps you feel it as a pulse.

The function of the blood vessels

(b) Name the three types of blood vessel and describe their functions.

(c) In which type of blood vessel does oxygenated blood normally travel?

(d) What is the one exception to (c) above?

Red and blue blood

(e) Deoxygenated blood is blue; you have only to look at the veins on the back of your hand to see this. So why is blood always red when you cut yourself?

You are as blue-blooded as the next duke.

Pulse rate

(f) Find pulse points on your wrist and temple. Take your own pulse now. Predict what will happen to your pulse after a brief spell of exercise.

(g) Explain why your pulse rate changes when you exercise.

The function of blood

(h) Blood is a mixture of the substances listed below. What function do these have?
- platelets
- phagocytes
- lymphocytes
- haemoglobin
- plasma

Lungs and gas exchange

(i) Blood carries oxygen to the cells of the body and carries away carbon dioxide. In what organ does gas exchange happen? What part do the following play in the process?
- capillaries
- oxygen
- alveoli
- bronchioles
- carbon dioxide

See more about cells in sections 4.14 and 4.15.

Transport to the cells

(j) What else does blood carry to the cells of the body?

Waste removal

(k) What else does blood carry away from the cells?

Blood is filtered in the kidneys.

(l) Which of the functions of the blood do you think children will find easiest to understand? Which one are they more likely to find difficult to accept?

....

4.5 Human movement

Skeleton

(a) Label as many of these bones as you can.

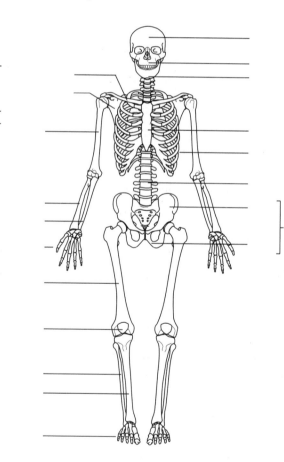

The skeleton can be regarded as a framework on which the muscles and organs hang.

Bones

(b) Which bones would you expect children to name at Key Stage 1?

(c) Are there any scientific names for bones you would expect children at Key Stage 2 to know?

Cartilage stops the bones from rubbing each other away. Ligaments hold the joints together.

Joints

(d) Name some joints which fall into these categories:
- ball and socket joints
- hinge joints
- sliding joints

Muscles

(e) What will happen when muscle A contracts?

Shoulder —

Muscle A

Elbow

Arm straight

(f) What is the meaning of the term 'antagonistic muscles'? Name some pairs of antagonistic muscles.

Muscle attachment

(g) How are muscles attached to the skeleton?

(h) Do a quick sketch showing a very simple model which children could make to demonstrate the way that muscles pull the forearm.

....

4.6 Human reproduction and growth

Reproduction parts

(a) What is the function of the following in reproduction?
- testes
- fallopian tubes
- placenta
- embryo
- ovaries
- uterus
- sperm
- foetus

An organ has a definite structure and function.

What is an organ?

(b) Which of the above are organs of the body?

In vitro fertilization

(c) How would you explain the process of _in vitro_ fertilization to an intelligent eleven-year-old?

In vitro literally means 'in glass.' There are many ethical issues concerning _in vitro_ fertilization.

....

4.7 Plant roots and stems

Roots grow downwards. They differ from stems in not having leaves or buds.

Roots

(a) What are the three functions of a root?

Tubers

(b) Why are potato tubers not roots? (Remember what happens to potatoes left in a cupboard.)

Potato tubers sprout in cool dark cupboards.

Bulbs

(c) How do you know that daffodil bulbs and onions are not roots? Explain your answer.

....

4.8 Leaves and photosynthesis

Photosynthesis

(a) What is the process of photosynthesis? Mention the different chemicals involved.

Simple chemical equation

(b) Write the simple chemical equation for what happens in a leaf during photosynthesis.

All organic materials contain the same elements.

(c) Can animals photosynthesize?

Plant food

(d) Plants obtain nutrients from the soil but many children incorrectly think that plants get food from the soil. Where do you think this mistaken idea might come from?

Respiration in plants

(e) Plants, like animals, produce the gas carbon dioxide. What is the process by which this happens?

4.9 Flowers

(a) Flowers are the structures that some plants use for reproduction.
Name the organs shown here.

Tulip

See section 6, Ecosystems and classification, for plants which do not flower.

(b) What are the male parts of a flower and what do they produce?

(c) What are the female parts and what do they produce?

(d) Which of the following are flowering plants?
- grass
- moss
- ivy
- seaweed
- oak tree
- birch tree
- fern

Explain your answer to each one.

All broadleaf deciduous trees flower. However, some do so early in the year or have very insignificant wind-pollinated flowers.

4.10 Health threats

(a) What are the main features of the following?
- viruses
- bacteria
- fungi

(b) Give three examples of how each can affect human health.

(c) Describe the health threats posed by mosquitoes in tropical countries.

For more detail on classification see section 6, Ecosystems and classification.

4.11 Healthy animals and plants

(a) What are the human body's first lines of defence against cuts becoming infected?

(b) How do immunizations and vaccinations work?

(c) Why do birds and mammals spend so much time grooming?

(d) Describe one pattern of behaviour which helps to rid a large animal of parasites.

Vaccinations were first used against smallpox.

4.12 Drugs and people

(a) What style of drug abuse is HIV infection associated with?

(b) What are the main constituents of tobacco smoke and what are their effects?

(c) Write down as many of the warnings on cigarette packets as you can remember.

(d) Name a disease against which these drugs, which are used as medicines, may be beneficial:
- antibiotics
- antihistamines
- fungicides
- aspirin

It is unlikely to be appropriate to discuss, with primary children, the way HIV is spread.

No drugs are effective against the viruses which cause colds and flu.

4.13 Healthy people

(a) Name three main classes of food and examples of each kind which are necessary for healthy growth.

Food provides energy and raw material.

Reproductive organs

Parts of a flower

Male parts

Female parts

Not all plants have flowers.

Micro-organisms

Infective agents

Parasites

Body defences

Immunity

Grooming behaviour

Parasite removal

HIV

Tobacco

Health warnings

Medicines

Types of food

Vitamins

Disability and health

Mental health

(b) What is the function of vitamins and how do we get them?

(c) What issues are raised in relation to disease and disability when talking with a class about 'good health'?

(d) Name and define two common mental illnesses.

(e) What class of disease accounts for the largest number of prescriptions?

Single cells

Plant and animal cells

Tissues and organs

4.14 Cells are us
(a) How big are cells? Are they:
- visible with the naked eye?
- visible using a magnifying glass?
- visible using a microscope?
- too small to be seen at all?

(b) Name some organisms which consist of only one single cell.

(c) What are the main differences between plant and animal cells?

(d) Give some examples of the types of cell which are in your body. Can you sketch any of them?

(e) Can you give an example of how cells group together in the body to form tissues and organs?

> Robert Hooke was the first person to recognize cells. He thought they resembled the small rooms occupied by monks.

Typical animal and plant cells

Cell nucleus

4.15 Cell structure
(a) Label this typical plant cell and animal cell.

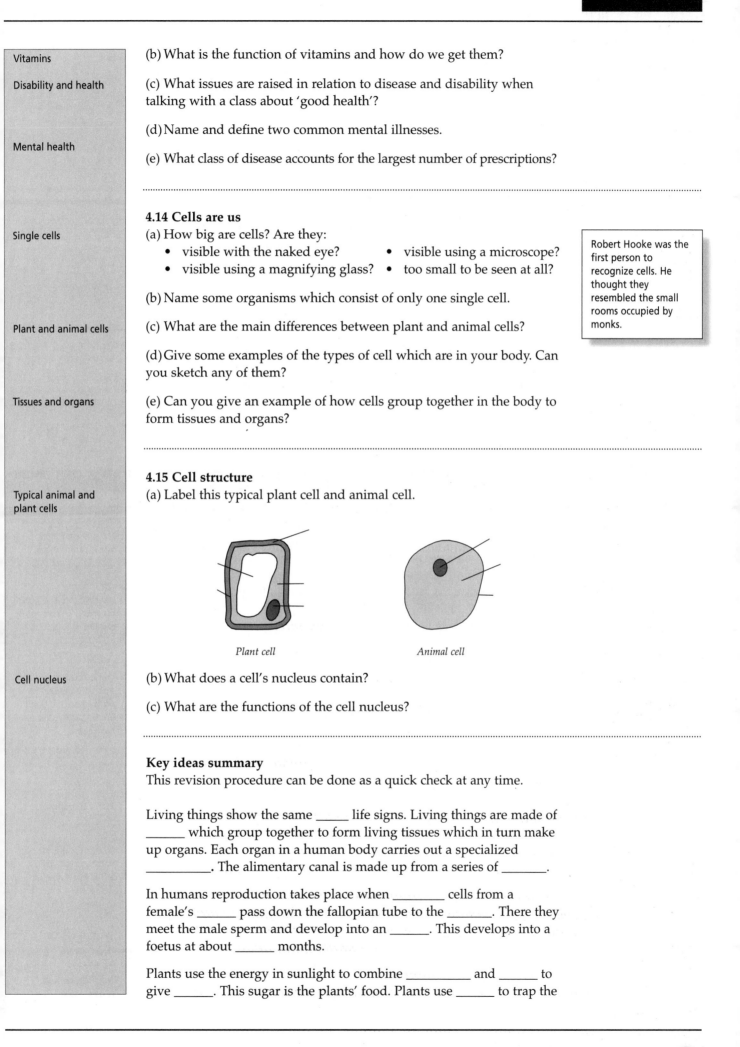

Plant cell   *Animal cell*

(b) What does a cell's nucleus contain?

(c) What are the functions of the cell nucleus?

Key ideas summary
This revision procedure can be done as a quick check at any time.

Living things show the same _____ life signs. Living things are made of _____ which group together to form living tissues which in turn make up organs. Each organ in a human body carries out a specialized _____. The alimentary canal is made up from a series of _____.

In humans reproduction takes place when _____ cells from a female's _____ pass down the fallopian tube to the _____. There they meet the male sperm and develop into an _____. This develops into a foetus at about _____ months.

Plants use the energy in sunlight to combine _____ and _____ to give _____. This sugar is the plants' food. Plants use _____ to trap the sun's light to power the chemical reaction of _____. Roots are the parts of plants which anchor the plant and draw up water and _____. Plants, in the same way as animals, respire when they break down _____ to power their life processes. Flowering plants reproduce when the female egg cell is _____ by the male pollen cell.

Human health is affected by a number of factors including _____ and environmental influences. Tobacco is one environmental factor which has a major effect on health. Micro-organisms including bacteria, _____, protozoa and _____ have health implications for people. Vaccination works against _____, such as flu and polio, by alerting the body to produce _____ against a later invasion. Antibiotics do not kill viruses and fungi – they are only effective against _____ such as meningitis or syphilis.

Cells comprise a _____ and other materials enclosed in a cell ___. Cell nuclei contain _____ which are made up from a series of genes, many of which programme the body to develop in different ways. All this ____ material is made from ____. This is a complex molecule which can replicate itself during cell division. Plant cells are much more robust than ____ cells because they are surrounded by a tough ____ wall. Plant cells also contain _____ which take part in photosynthesis.

5 Continuity and change

5.1 Life cycles and reproduction
(a) Which organisms are born looking like miniature versions of their parents?

See section 6.1 for classification details.

Insect life cycle words

(b) Define these words associated with an insect's life cycle.
- larva
- cocoon
- caterpillar
- chrysalis
- pupa
- metamorphosis
- maggot
- nymph

Insects have a complex life cycle. These words require accurate use.

Two different types of insect life cycles

(c) There are two types of insect life cycle. Describe them.

(d) Tick the plants from this list which reproduce using seeds.
- cactus
- seaweed
- moss
- mushroom
- pine tree
- fern
- dandelion

Think about the sort of structure needed to produce seeds. Many simple plants do not have seeds.

(e) How do the others reproduce?

5.2 Genes in cells
Genetic material

(a) Put these objects and materials into order of size. Write down what each one does.
- gene
- chromosome
- nucleus
- cell

Most older junior children will have heard of some of these words. Could you define each one accurately if asked by an intelligent 11-year-old?

Chromosomes

(b) What do you know about the chromosomes in every cell (except the sperm or egg cells) in your body?

Egg cells

(c) What is special about the chromosomes in your egg or sperm cells?

5.3 Genetics and reproduction
Clone

(a) What is a clone and why does this matter to Dolly?

Dolly is a famous Scottish sheep.

Genes

(b) Distinguish between these terms:
- dominant gene   • homozygous
- recessive gene   • heterozygous

(c) Why do children usually look like their parents?

Dominant and recessive characteristics

(d) One simple aspect of a trait is whether we can roll our tongue lengthways or not. Rolling (R) is dominant over not rolling (r). Say whether each of these individuals can roll their tongue or not.

> RR = a person who has both genes for rolling
> rr = a person who has both genes for not rolling
> Rr = a person who has one gene for rolling and one gene for not rolling

> Most traits are highly complex but the ability to tongue roll is fairly simple.

Eye colour

(e) The gene for blue eyes is recessive. What are the chances of having blue eyes if both parents are homozygous for blue eyes? What are the chances of having blue eyes if one parent has brown eyes (which is dominant over blue) and the other blue eyes?

> Draw a diagram showing the chances of inheriting a particular gene.

Inherited diseases

(f) Diseases like sickle cell anaemia and cystic fibrosis are recessive. How can a couple, both of whom are healthy, produce children affected by a disease like this?

> Other inherited diseases include haemophilia.

(g) Chromosomes split just before a cell divides. Normally each new cell gets two copies of the chromosome. What happens in the case of the sperm cell and the egg cell?

Intelligence

(h) Is intelligence inherited or acquired?

(i) What individuals would be good subjects for experiments into whether intelligence is inherited or acquired?

5.4 Evolution

Inherited or acquired?

(a) Which of these things can you inherit from your parents?
- the ability to speak English • a disease like haemophilia
- a big nose   • a disease like polio

Explain your ideas.

> 'Congenital' refers to conditions gained before birth (so it's unlikely that anyone is literally a 'congenital liar').

Darwin

(b) Which is Charles Darwin's most famous book?

(c) What is the theory he proposes in that book?

Backbones evolved only once.

(d) What do all vertebrates have in common? What support does this observation offer the theory of evolution?

(e) Humans have an appendix in the gut which in herbivores breaks down cellulose. Why do humans still have this apparently useless bit of gut?

> Humans have many left-over bits from their past. A lot of these are psychological.

(f) What does the study of vertebrate embryos tell us about the ancestors of all vertebrates?

Galapagos finches

(g) Darwin visited the Galapagos Islands and noted that many of the land birds seemed to be descended from a finch common in South America. How did he think that had happened?

Fossils

(h)

Sir David Attenborough considers it the world's most important fossil.

What is the special significance of the fossil called *Archaeopteryx*?

What is a species?

5.5 Species

(a) Define what constitutes a species.

Hybrids

(b) Horses can breed with donkeys to produce mules. So why are donkeys and horses still separate species?

Human hybrids?

(c) Why cannot humans and chimps be hybridized *in vitro*?

Even if this could be done would it be ethical?

Key ideas summary

This revision procedure can be done as a quick check at any time.

All living things go through _____ in their lives. Even humans which are born looking very like adults go through a great many changes before sexual _____. Most animals hatch from externally laid _____. Many insects have a complex life _____ which involves stages such as egg, _____ and _____. Corals and other sedentary animals have a _____ stage which can swim freely leading to new colonies.

Evolution occurs when the inevitable mistakes in DNA copying (mutation) lead to the occasional advantageous _____. The environment favours living things which are best equipped to exploit the available _____. Even a small _____ over an otherwise similar animal of the same species can lead to an individual's survival and ability to pass on _____ to the next generation.

Sickle cell anaemia and cystic fibrosis are examples of _____ diseases. Parents can be _____ of the disease gene but be unaware of this because the gene is _____ and they are heterozygous for the gene. Only if an adult has children by a similar _____ carrier may their children be _____ for that gene and therefore have the disease.

6 Ecosystems and classification

Classifying vertebrates

6.1 The classification of organisms

(a) Name the five groups of vertebrates.

(b) List the main characteristics of each vertebrate group.

'Arthritis' is a clue here.

Arthropods

(c) What is the meaning of the word arthropod?

(d) Which group of arthropods has six legs?

Beetles are a member of this group.

Eight-legged arthropods

(e) Which group of arthropods has eight legs?

(f) Which group of arthropods has more than eight legs?

Animals with five arms	(g) Which sea animals have five-rayed symmetry?
	(h) In what respect are fungi different from green plants?
Lichen	(i) What is a lichen?

Lichen	(i) What is a lichen?
The odd one out	(j) Identify the animal in each row which is the odd one out. Give reasons for your choice.

> Lichen are found in many harsh environments.

cow	man	trout
ostrich	tortoise	snake
seahorse	shark	lizard
spider	butterfly	grasshopper
crab	woodlouse	scorpion
toadstool	moss	dry rot

> This is a good game to play in the classroom.

6.2 Ecology words

Accurate vocabulary

(a) What is the meaning of the following words?
  • habitat • ecosystem • adaptation • ecology • environment

Give an example of each one.

Very small habitats

(b) Name some of the animals and plants which might live in or on a rotting log.

> Microhabitats can be very small.

(c) Name some of the animals and plants which might live in or on an oak tree.

A habitat may contain many organisms.

(d) Make lists of other assemblages (groups) of animals and plants which might be found in a single habitat.

Food chains

(e) In terms of food chains which words are being defined here?

An animal which eats other animals.
A plant which makes food by photosynthesis.
An animal which eats only plants.
A collective word for all animals in a food chain.

> Some animals eat plants and some eat other animals.

Why are there so few dangerous animals?

(f) What determines how much vegetation grows in an environment? How does this affect the number of big, dangerous animals in that environment?

(g) In what sense have plants made the world fit for animals?

(h) Are there any food chains which are **not** dependent on green plants?

> One of these occurs deep in the ocean.

6.3 Types of micro-organisms

Micro-organisms

(a) Name three examples of each of the following:
  • viruses • bacteria • protozoa • fungi

Compost

(b) A compost heap contains decomposing micro-organisms. What types are most important?

Sewage

(c) Sewage farms use bacteria to break down human waste. What are the end products of this process?

6.4 Humans affect their environment

Sulphur burning affects the environment.

(a) Coal and oil contain fairly large quantities of sulphur. What are the chemical and environmental consequences of burning sulphur?

Acid rain

(b) List some effects of acid rain. How could you reproduce the effects of acid rain in the classroom?

The greenhouse effect

(c) What causes the greenhouse effect? Can the greenhouse effect be thought of as a good thing?

(d) What are the possible consequences of the increasing greenhouse effect?

Ozone

(e) What is ozone?

The ozone layer

(f) Where is the ozone layer and what effect does ozone have in the atmosphere?

The hole in ozone layer

(g) What seems to be causing a depletion of the ozone layer? What effects will the depletion of the ozone layer have?

> Acid rain is natural; carbon dioxide and water forms carbonic acid.

> The physics of the greenhouse effect are clear but the causes and effects are hotly disputed.

Key ideas summary
This revision procedure can be done as a quick check at any time.

There is a huge variety of living things in the world. There are at least 40 million different _____. They are divided into groups which are based on their _____ history. For instance, sharks and dolphins are not considered to be closely _____ even though at first sight they look _____. Sharks and dolphins have quite distinct evolutionary histories with sharks being related to other _____ and dolphins being _____.

Food chains show which animals feed on which plants and animals. All food chains, except those round deep _____ vents and deep inside the rocks of the continents, start with a _____ plant.

The greenhouse effect is vital to life on the planet. However, the enhanced greenhouse effect caused by industry may create changes which will bring dramatic _____ changes. The depletion of the ozone layer is caused by chemicals released by people. These _____ with ozone in the _____ atmosphere allowing more _____ light to reach the Earth's surface.

7 Particle theory

7.1 Particles

Particle size

(a) Put these particles in order of size:
- atom
- molecule
- electron
- atomic nucleus

Atom

(b) What is an atom?

(c)

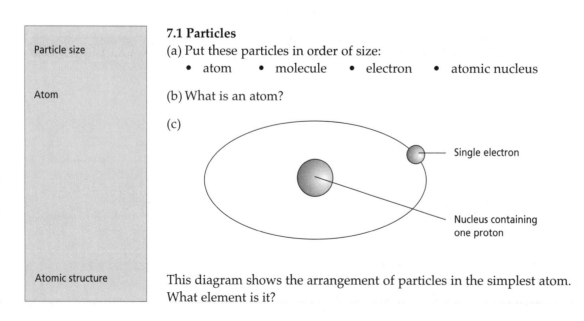

Single electron

Nucleus containing one proton

Atomic structure

This diagram shows the arrangement of particles in the simplest atom. What element is it?

> The structure of atoms was worked out early in the twentieth century.

Electron

Ion

(d) What is an electron?

(e) What is an ion?

(f) Is it possible to grind powders so fine that each tiny fragment is a single molecule or atom?

7.2 Chemical bonding

Bonding

(a) A chemical bond holds atoms or ions together. Which types of bond do you know about? Draw simple diagrams of the chemical bonds between sodium and chlorine, and carbon and hydrogen.

Glucose

(b) Glucose is the sugar which is most important in our diets. Write down the chemical formula for a glucose molecule.

> See section 4.8 (b) on photosynthesis.

Starch

(c) Starch consists of glucose molecules linked together in a long chain. What does the body have to do to the chain before it can get the energy from the starch?

Fats

(d) What elements are fats made from?

Energy drinks

(e) Why do athletes who want almost instant energy drink glucose and not milk?

Dense energy

(f) Why do polar explorers eat a great deal of fat and relatively little pasta?

> See section 8.2 for information on how glucose is broken down.

Key ideas summary

This revision procedure can be done as a quick check at any time.

All _____ is made up from atoms. Atoms consist of a large number of particles that include _____ and neutrons which form the nucleus and _____ which orbit the nucleus. An _____ is a charged particle which has lost or gained an electron. _____ bond together to form molecules

_____ are made up from one sort of atom. _____ are made up from two or more sorts of atoms bonded together.

8 Materials

8.1 Elements and compounds

Elements

(a) Define what is meant by an element.

Compounds

(b) Define what is meant by a compound.

(c) Which of these are elements and which are compounds?
- copper
- sulphur
- rust
- sugar
- uranium
- hydrochloric acid
- iron
- argon
- carbon dioxide
- water
- salt
- zinc
- arsenic

> Very few metals are found naturally as elements.

(d) Can you separate any compounds simply by dissolving them in water and then allowing the water to evaporate?

Molecules

(e) What is a molecule? Can molecules contain atoms of more than one element?

Elements react to give compounds.

(f) What compound can be formed when these two elements combine?
- hydrogen and oxygen
- silicon and oxygen
- carbon and oxygen
- sulphur and oxygen
- sodium and chlorine

What is wax?

8.2 Chemical reactions

(a) Candle wax is a compound of two elements. Fuels like wax are known as hydrocarbons. What two elements make up hydrocarbon fuels?

Fuels

(b) Name some other hydrocarbon fuels.

Burning reactions

(c) When a candle burns it produces two main products. Write the word equations for the burning reaction.

> When fuels burn they combine with oxygen.

(d) Write the chemical equation for the burning reaction of methane gas.

Candle wick myths

(e) Many children think that wax is only in a candle to hold up the wick. They think the wax itself does little or no burning. What might cause them to hold that misconception?

Reversible burning?

(f) If you were to burn 5 gm of wax would the gases produced by the burning have a greater or a lesser mass than the original wax?

(g) The programme of study for Key Stage 2 suggests that **most** burning is not reversible. Name **one** burning reaction which is reversible and say how it can be reversed.

> Water is the clue here.

Respiration

(h) When you digest food, chemical reactions happen in your body. What are the main products of these reactions?

Plant reactions

(i) What is the chemical reaction which traps energy from sunlight?

(j) Why is it true to say that the chemical reaction mentioned in (i) is reversed by our bodies?

> See section 4 for information on life processes.

Melting and evaporating

8.3 Physical changes: melting, freezing, evaporating and dissolving

(a) Explain the energy transfers involved in the change from ice to water to water vapour.

(b) Interpret the graph below and suggest why it show flat areas at the points at which water is changing state.

Temperature of a pan of ice as it is steadily heated

Molecules of water	(c) Do the oxygen and hydrogen atoms come apart at any point in the above changes?

Water behaves oddly as it cools. Remember that ice floats on water.

Why does ice float?

(d) What happens to the spacing of water molecules in the changes from ice to water to water vapour?

Evaporation

(e) In which ways can you speed evaporation?

Dissolving

(f) These words are associated with dissolving. Define each word and give an example of the correct use of each.
- solution
- suspension
- emulsion
- solvent
- colloid
- saturated

All the words associated with dissolving need careful definition.

Re-crystallization

(g) When salt dissolves in water, how can you get the salt back?

If it were possible to filter salt then water shortages would be a thing of the past.

Filtration

(h) Why is it not possible to filter salt particles from a solution using a very fine filter?

Suspensions

(i) When you mix flour in water how do you know the flour is suspended in the water and has not dissolved?

(j) What accounts for the fact that many children think that flour dissolves in water?

Just mixing in isn't enough.

(k) Explain the physical changes to coffee which take place:

when you make a pot of filter coffee
if you let the coffee pot dry out
if you add water to the dried-out remains.

Even instant coffee is made from ground beans in the first place.

8.4 The properties of solids, liquids and gases

Three states of matter

(a) Which one material exists naturally on the Earth as a solid, a liquid and a gas?

(b) Define:
- gas
- liquid
- solid

Gases are material even though most are invisible.

(c) How could you find out if a gas has weight?

8.5 Physical changes

Physical changes

(a) Match one of these words to one of the sentences below:
- condense
- melt
- solidify
- evaporation
- dissolve
- liquefy

All physical changes are reversible.

This process happens in fridges if you leave bread uncovered.
A drop in temperature causes water vapour to do this.
The metal lead does this at 600°C.
Lard does this when cooled to room temperature.
Salt does this but sand does not.
Sand will do this at very high temperatures, as in the glass making process.

It is important to clarify the distinction between 'melting' and 'dissolving'.

Melting/dissolving

(b) Explain and give examples of the difference between melting and dissolving.

Key ideas summary

This revision procedure can be done as a quick check at any time.

Compounds are the result of _____ reactions and they require another reaction to split them apart. _____ is one sort of chemical reaction.

This happens when a fuel is combined with oxygen. _____ is a compound made from burning the element hydrogen in oxygen.

The properties of solids can be explained by the idea that the particles are _____ attracted to each other. There are ___ forces between the particles of gas. When gas cools it _____ into a liquid.

A solid which dissolves in a liquid is a _____. The mixture of this solid and a solvent is a _____. A _____ is a mixture of a liquid and fine undissolved particles.

9 Electricity and magnetism

9.1 Conductors and insulators

Conductors

Insulators

(a) Name some good conductors of electricity.

(b) Name some materials which will not let electricity pass through them.

Resistors

(c) Name some materials which will conduct electricity but will not let it pass through them easily.

Explaining conduction

(d) Explain why some materials are good conductors and others are insulators.

> Most materials which conduct electricity also conduct heat well.

> See section 7.1, Particles.

9.2 Current and flow

Flow of electricity

(a) Explain what you understand by the term 'flow of electricity'.

An analogy for electrical flow

(b) The flow of electricity can be compared to a central heating system.

> Refer back to the information on electrons in 9.1 (d).

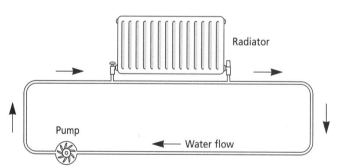

Why is the battery likened to the pump?

Electrons

(c) Electrons are negatively charged. Use that information to explain which way electrons are being pushed around the circuit below.

> Like charges repel and unlike charges attract.

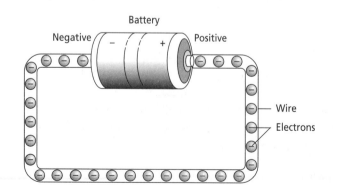

The flow of electricity is the same throughout a series circuit.

(d)

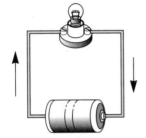
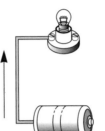

How do you know that the flow of electrons has to be the same throughout a simple circuit like this?

Ammeters and electrical flow

How electricity flows

(e) Ammeters measure electrical flow. What unit do they measure this in?

(f) Which of these diagrams is the correct explanation of the way in which electrical flow works?

Osborne and Freyberg (1985) used these diagrams to probe children's under-standing.

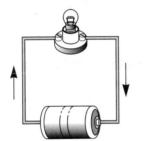
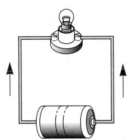

The current flow is less in the return wire

The return wire is not needed

The current is the same whether the wire is going to or returning from the bulb

The current moves along both wires and clashes in the middle causing the bulb to light

Potential difference

9.3 Voltage

(a) What is voltage?

(b) Describe how voltage is measured.

(c) Describe any analogy you have heard which helps to explain the concept of voltage.

Match the voltage of bulb and battery.

(d)

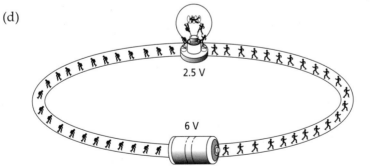

2.5 V

6 V

Why is it a bad idea to use a 6-volt battery with a 2.5-volt bulb? Explain what will happen to the filament of the bulb. Use the idea of energy in your explanation.

In classrooms, standardize on one voltage. (See the companion volume, *Teaching Science in Primary Schools*, for details.)

Electrical energy

(e) What SI unit is used to measure electrical energy?

9.4 Resistance

Electrical flow through conductors

(a) Draw one picture to show how you think electricity passes through a good conductor and another to show how you think electricity flows through a poor conductor.

Drawing your ideas can help you to understand them more clearly.

The parts of a bulb

(b) Label this diagram of a bulb.

Bulbs are filled with inert gases so the filament does not combine with oxygen. See section 8.4.

How a bulb works

(c) Explain how a bulb works.

Copper wire and tungsten filament

(d) Contrast the way in which electricity flows through copper wires with the way it flows through a bulb filament.

A puzzling series circuit

(e) In a lesson on circuits a child puts two non-identical bulbs in series; one is rated 1.5 V and the other is rated 3.5 V. She notices that one glows more brightly than the other. Which of the following is the best explanation for this?

the electricity goes to one bulb first and that uses most of it up
the bulb with the greater resistance glows more brightly.

(f) What simple test could you undertake to investigate this idea?

Unit of resistance

(g) What is the SI unit of resistance?

Series and parallel circuits

(h) In which of the circuits below are the bulbs wired in series and in which are they wired in parallel?

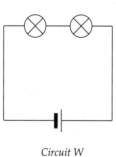

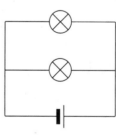

Check the symbols in section 9.6 (a) below

Circuit W   *Circuit X*

The brightness of the bulbs will differ.

(i) Assuming all the bulbs are identical, in which of the circuits will the bulbs glow more brightly?

(j) In each circuit what will happen if one of the bulbs is unscrewed? Explain your answer.

The current flowing will depend on the resistance.

(k) In which circuit is more current flowing through each bulb? Explain your answer using a diagram and arrows.

See section 9.2 when answering. Which circuit will have more resistance?

9.5 Power

Electrical energy

(a) Electrical energy can be changed into other forms of energy. Other forms of energy can be changed into electricity. Give some examples of energy changes involving electricity.

> Energy is never destroyed or used up. Most energy changes end up in heat.

Different rates of energy use

(b) Put these in order from most to least electricity used per minute.
- electric kettle
- torch
- light bulb
- pocket calculator

> The greater the power an electrical item has the more noise, light, heat or movement it will produce.

Power

(c) Define the word 'power'.

River analogy

(d) Write down how electrical power is calculated. Think of an analogy involving water flow in a river.

Torch bulb power

(e) Which of these torch bulbs uses most power?

Kilowatt

(f) How many watts are there in a kilowatt (kW)?

What does it cost you?

(g) A one bar (1 kW) electric fire uses a unit of electricity every hour. One unit costs 6p. How much does it cost to:

> Use this information to work out the power of the items you use. Find out how much power your TV uses on standby.

light a 100 W bulb for an hour?
light a 60 W bulb for 5 hours?
light a 10 W energy saver bulb for two days (50 hours)?
heat a 3 kW kettle for 6 minutes?
have a 10 kW shower for 12 minutes?

Calculating watts

(h) How much money would you save in a year if you used a 20 watt energy saving bulb instead of a 100 W bulb? (Assume you used it 5 hours per day and the extra cash price of the energy saving bulb was £6.)

> This is practical advice.

9.6 Circuit symbols and diagrams

Circuit symbols

(a) Write down next to each of the symbols below the name of the electrical device represented. Annotate the circuit diagram in the same way.

> Introduce circuit symbols and diagrams once the children are confident with doing representational drawings.

Circuit diagram

> A single cylindrical battery is more correctly called a cell.

Series circuit

(b) Draw a circuit diagram showing two bulbs in series with a switch and a 6 V battery.

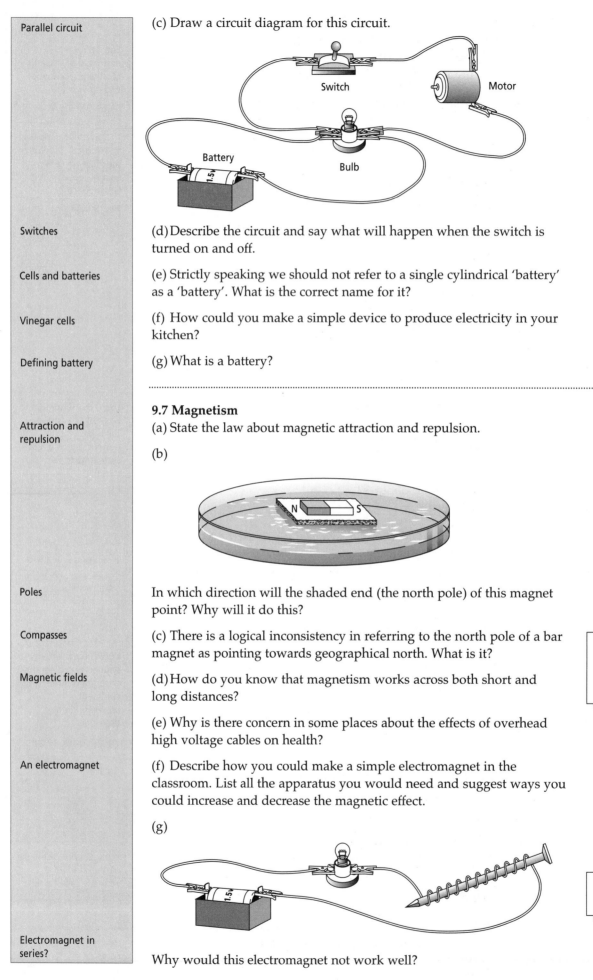

Parallel circuit

(c) Draw a circuit diagram for this circuit.

Switch

Motor

Battery

Bulb

Switches

(d) Describe the circuit and say what will happen when the switch is turned on and off.

Cells and batteries

(e) Strictly speaking we should not refer to a single cylindrical 'battery' as a 'battery'. What is the correct name for it?

Vinegar cells

(f) How could you make a simple device to produce electricity in your kitchen?

Defining battery

(g) What is a battery?

9.7 Magnetism

(a) State the law about magnetic attraction and repulsion.

Attraction and repulsion

(b)

N   S

Poles

In which direction will the shaded end (the north pole) of this magnet point? Why will it do this?

Compasses

(c) There is a logical inconsistency in referring to the north pole of a bar magnet as pointing towards geographical north. What is it?

It is illogical to call the end of a magnet which points north, the north pole.

Magnetic fields

(d) How do you know that magnetism works across both short and long distances?

(e) Why is there concern in some places about the effects of overhead high voltage cables on health?

An electromagnet

(f) Describe how you could make a simple electromagnet in the classroom. List all the apparatus you would need and suggest ways you could increase and decrease the magnetic effect.

(g)

Remember that bulbs are resistors.

Electromagnet in series?

Why would this electromagnet not work well?

(h) How could you detect the small magnetic effect of a single, nearly flat, battery?

Even a small flow will produce magnetism.

Key ideas summary

This revision procedure can be done as a quick check at any time.

_____ are involved in carrying electrical charge through a _____. If they encounter difficulty in flowing the material is a poor conductor of charge. Poor conductors are referred to as _____. When a current passes through a poor conductor the material heats up and may glow white hot. This happens usefully in a bulb _____. A _____ pushes electrons round a circuit – the force of the push is measured in _____ and the amount of flow is measured in _____. The power of a current is found by multiplying the flow (____) by the force (____) to give power in watts. Low energy light bulbs operate at the same _____ as ordinary light bulbs (240 volts) but they allow only relatively small flows of electricity through them.

Magnetic effect can be produced by a _____ flowing in a wire. Magnets have two poles. Like poles of a magnet _____.

10 Energy

10.1 Energy, force and fuel

Examples of force, fuel and energy

(a) In each of the following identify the force, the fuel and the energy:

    a man pushing a car
    the wind turning a windmill
    a rocket taking off.

Which SI units are used to measure force, fuel and energy?

SI units are described on page 51.

Body fuel

(b) What fuel do you use in your body?

10.2 Generating electricity

Power station

(a) Describe the stages by which electricity is produced in a fossil fuel power station.

Fossil fuels are trapped sunlight.

Types of energy

(b) Describe the same stages using these words in your account:
    chemical energy   kinetic energy
    heat energy   electrical energy

Energy changes

Nuclear power

(c) How does uranium drive power stations?

10.3 Biological and chemical energy

Energy changes in a candle

(a) When chemical bonds are broken, energy is released. Give an example of this process as it happens when a candle burns.

See section 7.2, Chemical bonding,

Plant energy

(b) What are the two main energy changes which happen in plants?

Calculating food energy

(c) What method is used to calculate the energy value of food?

Think of oily foods.

(d) How could you model this method in the classroom?

10.4 Energy resources

Types of energy

(a) There are many types of energy. Define and give one example of each of these:
- kinetic energy
- chemical energy
- gravitational potential energy
- strain potential energy
- heat energy

Energy changes always end up with heat.

Energy changes

(b) Describe the sequence of energy changes which take place when and just after a stone is fired into the air from a catapult.

Fossil fuels will eventually run out. When this starts to happen their price will rise dramatically. Current prices are steady or falling (1998).

Which fuels are renewable?

(c) Which of these is a fossil fuel? Which is a renewable resource?
- wood
- oil
- wind
- coal
- sugar cane
- peat

Burnt fuel

(d) Explain why when you burn a fuel you cannot concentrate it into a useful form again.

Key ideas summary

This revision procedure can be done as a quick check at any time.

Energy can be _____ from one form into another. You power your body with _____ energy (food) which is turned into movement, noise and heat. All the food energy is eventually dissipated as _____. It is difficult to reconcentrate the _____ again. Energy in the form of _____ can be burnt to produce heat to make steam (moving energy) which makes _____ in generators.

Another sequence of energy changes can be found in a catapult: food – _____ – elastic strain energy – _____ – heat (friction) and _____ (which changes into heat from the friction between the air molecules.

11 Forces

11.1 Measuring force

Unit of force

(a) Which SI unit is used to measure force?

It is named after a famous English scientist.

Simple calculations

(b) How much force is needed to hold up:

an apple which has a mass of 100 g?
a book with a mass of 300 g?

An average apple has a mass of 100 g.

Work

(c) Work is measured in joules. Work = force × distance moved. How much work is done:

lifting a mass of 500 g upwards by 2 metres?
dragging a bag 3 metres along the floor with a force of 4 newtons?

See joule in section 10.1 (a).

A working definition

11.2 Balanced forces

How can you recognize balanced forces?

(a) Give an example of when you have moved at a constant speed and felt no pushes and pulls.

The sensation of changing forces on your own body helps you make sense of forces.

(b) In which of the following situations are the forces balanced? What forces are operating in each case?

Are these balanced?

a boat floating
a hot air balloon hovering

Learn this simple way of knowing if forces on an object are balanced.

Balanced forces are at work when an object is
- still
- moving at a constant speed.

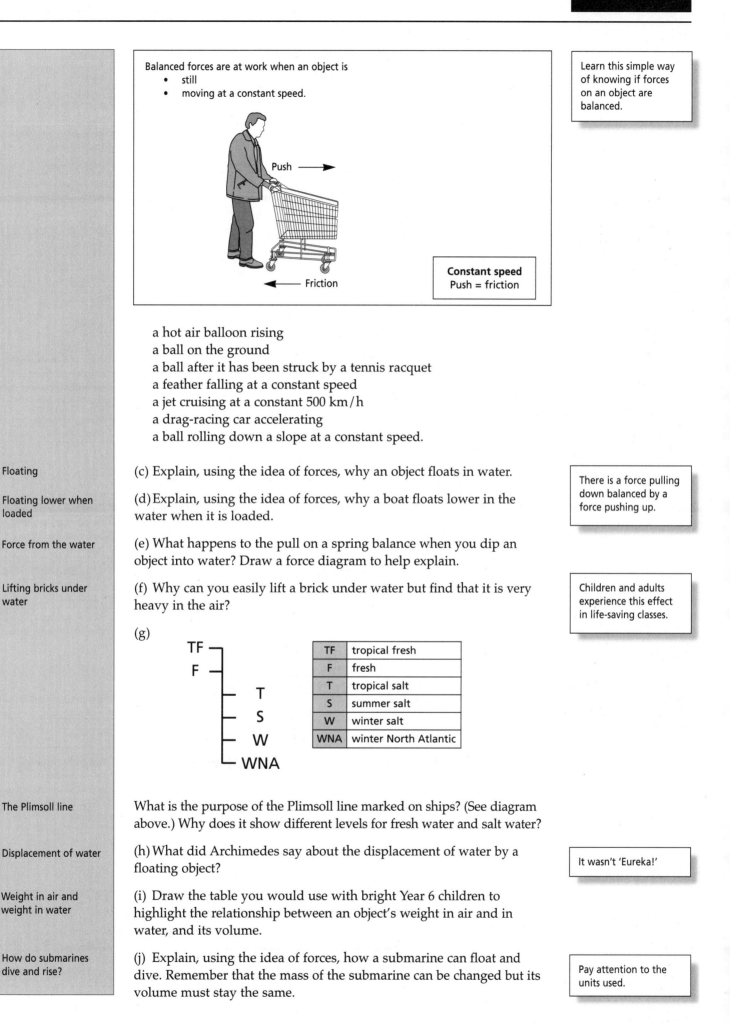

Push →

← Friction

Constant speed
Push = friction

a hot air balloon rising
a ball on the ground
a ball after it has been struck by a tennis racquet
a feather falling at a constant speed
a jet cruising at a constant 500 km/h
a drag-racing car accelerating
a ball rolling down a slope at a constant speed.

Floating

(c) Explain, using the idea of forces, why an object floats in water.

There is a force pulling down balanced by a force pushing up.

Floating lower when loaded

(d) Explain, using the idea of forces, why a boat floats lower in the water when it is loaded.

Force from the water

(e) What happens to the pull on a spring balance when you dip an object into water? Draw a force diagram to help explain.

Lifting bricks under water

(f) Why can you easily lift a brick under water but find that it is very heavy in the air?

Children and adults experience this effect in life-saving classes.

(g)

TF
F

T

S

W

WNA

TF	tropical fresh
F	fresh
T	tropical salt
S	summer salt
W	winter salt
WNA	winter North Atlantic

The Plimsoll line

What is the purpose of the Plimsoll line marked on ships? (See diagram above.) Why does it show different levels for fresh water and salt water?

Displacement of water

(h) What did Archimedes say about the displacement of water by a floating object?

It wasn't 'Eureka!'

Weight in air and weight in water

(i) Draw the table you would use with bright Year 6 children to highlight the relationship between an object's weight in air and in water, and its volume.

How do submarines dive and rise?

(j) Explain, using the idea of forces, how a submarine can float and dive. Remember that the mass of the submarine can be changed but its volume must stay the same.

Pay attention to the units used.

A definition

11.3 Unbalanced forces

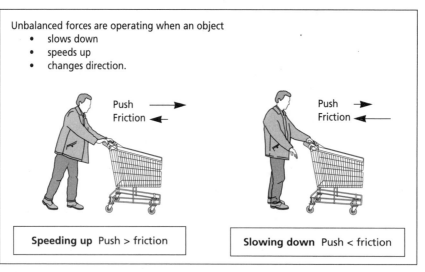

Unbalanced forces are operating when an object
- slows down
- speeds up
- changes direction.

Push ⟶
Friction ⟵

Push ⟶
Friction ⟵

Speeding up Push > friction

Slowing down Push < friction

Feel the force

(a) Describe occasions when travelling when you have felt unbalanced forces on you.

You can feel an unbalanced force, particularly on take-off in an aircraft.

Spot the unbalanced forces.

(b) Look at these three diagrams. Describe the forces acting on the ball in each of them. Are the forces balanced or unbalanced in each diagram? Explain your ideas.

Once the hand is no longer touching the ball, nothing is pushing it up.

Ball leaves hand   *Reaches top of flight*   *Falls*

Unbalanced forces?

(c) In which of these situations are the forces unbalanced? Describe the forces acting in each case.

- a golf ball sitting on the tee
- a golf ball in the process of being hit
- a golf ball just after being hit
- a golf ball rolling to a standstill on the green
- a ballet dancer on points
- a dancer leaping
- a trolley being pushed at a constant speed
- a trolley rolling to a standstill

Remember how to recognize balanced and unbalanced forces.

Upward forces in a swimming pool

(d) Which force makes it difficult to hold a large beach ball under water? Draw the forces on a beachball being held under water. What happens when you let go of the ball?

Forces on a party balloon

(e) What will happen to a party balloon filled with helium if you let go of it out of doors? Describe the forces which operate on it.

How do you know the forces are unbalanced?

Balancing the forces on the balloon

(f) Describe, in terms of forces, how you could make a helium party balloon stay on the floor without tying it down.

(g) Describe how you could make a free-floating helium party balloon hover at eye level and not rise to the ceiling or sink to the floor.

11.4 Friction

Measuring friction

(a) How would you measure the amount of friction between a box and a carpet?

Brakes

(b) How is friction used to slow a bicycle?

Friction enables walking

(c) If there were no friction why would you not be able to walk?

(d) Draw the diagram of the foot of a walking person and the ground, with arrows showing the direction of push and friction.

11.5 Air resistance

Dropping sheets of paper

(a) Get two pieces of scrap paper. Screw one up into a ball and drop it. Compare the speed of its fall with that of dropping a flat piece of paper. What do you notice? Explain this in terms of forces.

Free-falling parachutes

(b) Draw in the forces of gravity and air resistance in these diagrams.

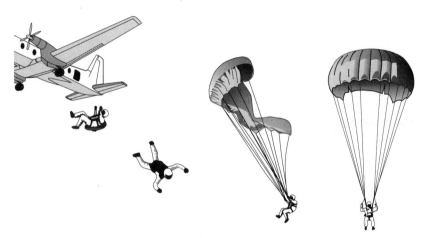

(i) Leaving airplane   *(ii) Terminal velocity*   *(iii) Parachute opens*   *(iv) Terminal velocity with parachute*

(c) Explain how you know that the forces in diagrams (*i*) and (*iii*) are unbalanced.

(d) Explain how you know the forces in (*ii*) and (*iv*) are balanced.

Counter-intuitive ideas

(e) Why do people find the idea of balanced forces in (*ii*) and (*iv*) difficult to accept?

11.6 Mass, gravity and weight

Defining mass, weight and gravity

(a) Define the following words:
- mass
- weight
- gravity

Moon mass

(b) What would happen to your mass on the moon?

Moon weight

(c) What would happen to your weight on the moon? How do you know that astronauts are not weightless on the moon?

Jupiter weight

(d) What would happen to your weight if you could stand on Jupiter?

(e) Pick up a paperclip and a heavy book. Which is pulled harder by gravity? If both are dropped at the same time, which would hit the ground first?

(f) Galileo was reputed to have dropped a large cannon ball and a small musket ball from the Tower of Pisa. Which would hit the ground first if both were dropped at the same time?

....

11.7 Speed, acceleration, distance and time

(a) What is the average speed of a car which travels 100 km in 2 hours?

(b) Look at this graph. When was the car accelerating rapidly? When was it accelerating slowly? How do you know?

> Velocity is speed in a particular direction.

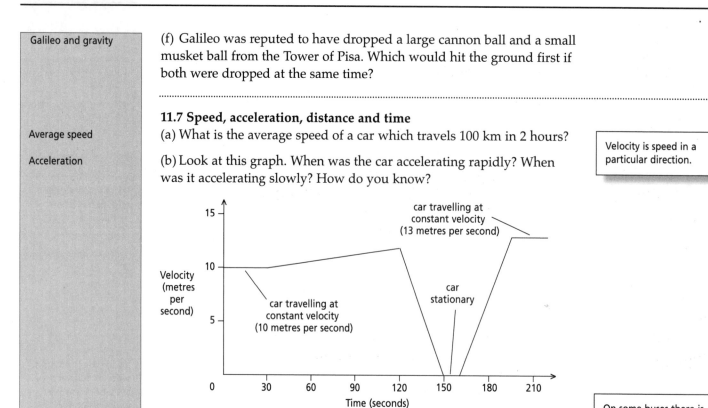

(c) Use the example of a bus journey to help explain the difference between speed and acceleration.

> On some buses there is low speed and even less acceleration.

....

Key ideas summary
This revision procedure can be done as a quick check at any time.

A _____ is a push or a pull. If all the forces acting on an object are _____ then the object stays still or moves at a constant speed in a constant direction. A stationary train has _____ forces acting on it. The same train travelling at a _____ speed in a straight line also has balanced forces acting on it. Passengers do not feel pulls and pushes when the train is travelling at a constant speed nor when it is _____. Objects which are floating in air or in _____ have _____ forces acting on them.

_____ forces operate when the pulls or pushes are bigger in one direction than in another. This results in the object speeding up or _____ down. As a train accelerates or slows down passengers can feel the change in the forces on them.

_____ pulls on masses. Mass is measured in grams and _____. The pull of gravity on these masses is called _____ and is measured in _____. Objects such as iron balls, which are fairly heavy for their surface area, will fall at the _____ speed if dropped from a fairly tall building. Air _____ is a force which _____ moving objects. This has more effect on light objects as they fall through the ____ than it does on heavy objects.

When an object is placed in water it _____ some of the water. This is true both for objects which _____ and those which float. When an object displaces water it is pushed up or supported by the ____. This is true for floaters and sinkers. This 'push up' is called _____ or upthrust. The amount of upthrust is the same as the _____ __ _____ which is displaced by the object. This is true for floaters and sinkers.

An object which floats in water experiences an upthrust which is ____ to its total weight. A floater is effectively weightless. The forces of _____ and upthrust are in balance An object which sinks in water loses some _____. The weight lost by a sinker is equal to the weight of the water which the sinker _____.

12 Light

12.1 Light travels

Straight lines and light

(a) What pieces of evidence can you use to demonstrate that light travels in straight lines? List at least two.

See section 14.3 on eclipses.

Shadows

(b) Explain how shadows are formed.

Umbra and penumbra

(c) Look in your room. Sketch a shadow and label the umbra and penumbra.

12.2 Colour and the properties of light

What is light?

(a) Light is part of the electromagnetic spectrum of radiation. Sketch out a spectrum of all the forms of radiation from gamma rays to radio waves.

Some animals see objects using reflected light from parts of the spectrum not visible to us.

Ultraviolet and infra-red

(b) On this spectrum of light label where you would expect to find ultraviolet and infra-red. What type of radiation is at these positions?

(c) What are the literal meanings of 'ultraviolet' and 'infra-red'?

Primary colours

(d) What are the three primary colours **of light**?

Primary colours differ in art and science.

Filters

(e) What effect would you notice if you looked (i) through a red filter, (ii) through a blue filter?

(f)

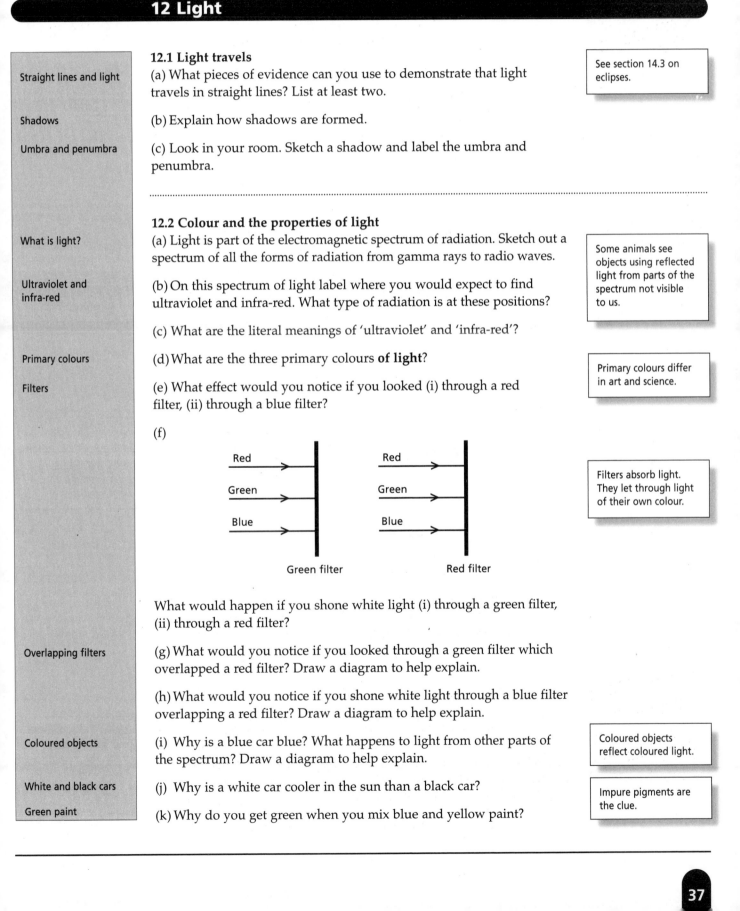

Green filter   Red filter

Filters absorb light. They let through light of their own colour.

What would happen if you shone white light (i) through a green filter, (ii) through a red filter?

Overlapping filters

(g) What would you notice if you looked through a green filter which overlapped a red filter? Draw a diagram to help explain.

(h) What would you notice if you shone white light through a blue filter overlapping a red filter? Draw a diagram to help explain.

Coloured objects

(i) Why is a blue car blue? What happens to light from other parts of the spectrum? Draw a diagram to help explain.

Coloured objects reflect coloured light.

White and black cars

(j) Why is a white car cooler in the sun than a black car?

Green paint

(k) Why do you get green when you mix blue and yellow paint?

Impure pigments are the clue.

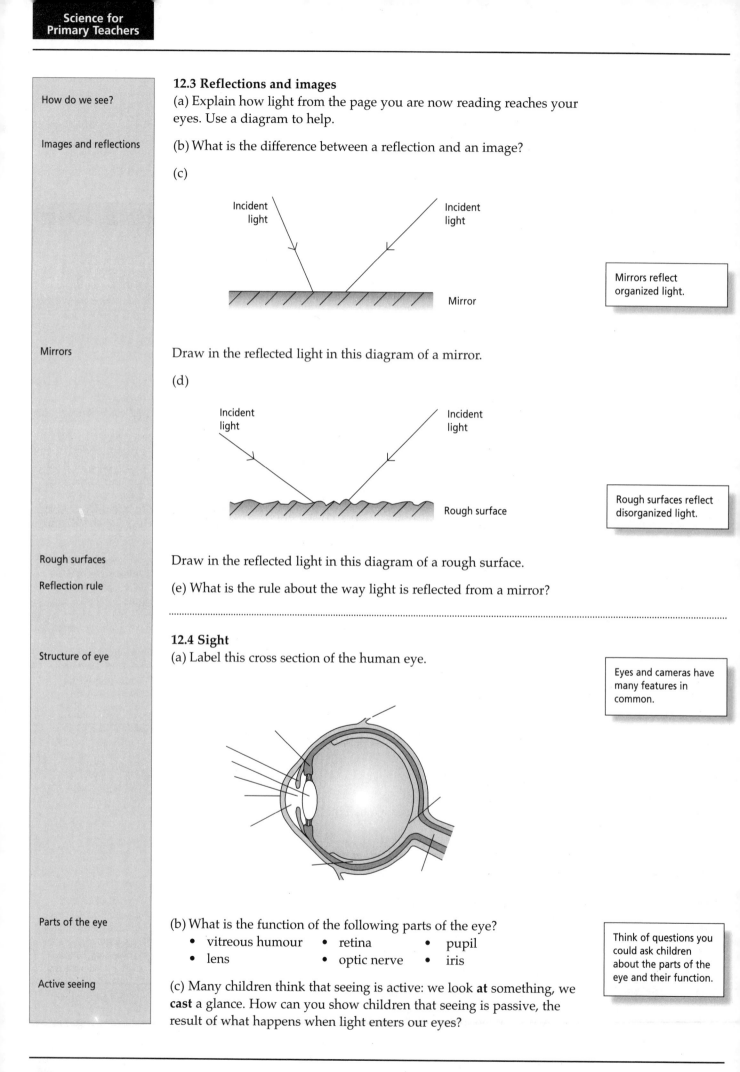

How do we see?

Images and reflections

Mirrors

Rough surfaces

Reflection rule

Structure of eye

Parts of the eye

Active seeing

12.3 Reflections and images

(a) Explain how light from the page you are now reading reaches your eyes. Use a diagram to help.

(b) What is the difference between a reflection and an image?

(c)

Incident light

Incident light

Mirror

Mirrors reflect organized light.

Draw in the reflected light in this diagram of a mirror.

(d)

Incident light

Incident light

Rough surface

Rough surfaces reflect disorganized light.

Draw in the reflected light in this diagram of a rough surface.

(e) What is the rule about the way light is reflected from a mirror?

12.4 Sight

(a) Label this cross section of the human eye.

Eyes and cameras have many features in common.

(b) What is the function of the following parts of the eye?
- vitreous humour
- retina
- pupil
- lens
- optic nerve
- iris

Think of questions you could ask children about the parts of the eye and their function.

(c) Many children think that seeing is active: we look **at** something, we **cast** a glance. How can you show children that seeing is passive, the result of what happens when light enters our eyes?

12.5 Lenses

(a) How can you focus an image of a window or a candle on to a piece of paper using a lens?

> Hold the lens a little way from the paper.

(b) In what way is this similar to what happens in the eye?

Focusing an image with a lens

Key ideas summary

This revision procedure can be done as a quick check at any time.

Light travels in _____ lines. Where it is blocked _____ are formed. We see objects because light from a source is _____ off them into our eyes. Mirrors reflect _____ – these are reflected pictures of an object.

Visible light is just one small part of the full spectrum of _____ radiation. Radio waves are very _____ waves and x-rays are very _____ wave radiation from this spectrum. Different coloured light has different _____. Red has _____ waves than blue. Infra-red radiation is heat and ultraviolet rays _____ skin in sunlight.

Red objects look red because they reflect only _____ light and absorb the other primary _____. When we look at white paper through a blue _____ it appears blue because the filter absorbs the other _____ colours and lets through blue only.

13 Sound

13.1 Vibrations and travelling sound

(a) How do you know that sound can travel through the following materials?
  • air • water • steel • wood • brick

> Sound travels faster and better through solids than it does through the air.

(b) How do astronauts communicate with each other on the moon?

> Even when they are just inches apart astronauts on the moon need radios.

(c) Evelyn Glennie is a world famous percussionist. She is completely deaf. How can she play percussion instruments accurately?

(d) Explain how these instruments make sound:
  • trombone • organ • violin • triangle • oboe

Sound travels through things.

Communicating on the moon

A deaf musician

Instruments

13.2 Loudness and pitch

(a) Define the following words:
  • volume • amplitude • pitch • frequency

(b) List the factors which affect the pitch of a vibrating string.

> There are three factors.

(c) What factor affects the pitch of an organ tube?

(d) How can a percussionist change the pitch of a drum?

(e) How can a percussionist use a file to affect the pitch of a xylophone key?

(f) Look at this pattern of sound waves.
Label the places where the sound is:
  • loud • high pitched
  • quiet • low pitched

> This way of representing sound waves is diagrammatic. It is not a good way of showing children how sound travels.

Pitch and volume definitions

String pitch

Organ pitch

Drum pitch

Block pitch

Sound waves

Parts of the ear

13.3 Hearing
(a)

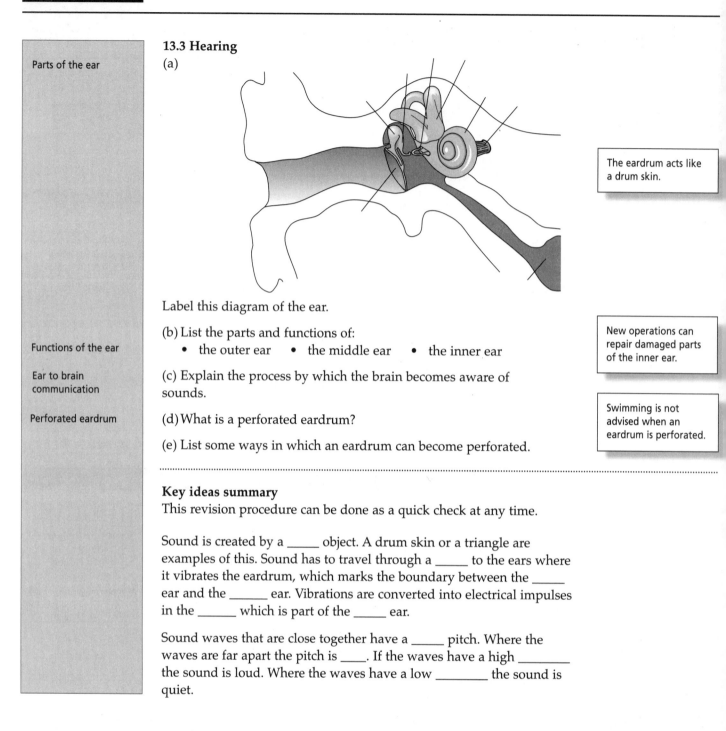

The eardrum acts like a drum skin.

Label this diagram of the ear.

(b) List the parts and functions of:
* the outer ear
* the middle ear
* the inner ear

Functions of the ear

(c) Explain the process by which the brain becomes aware of sounds.

Ear to brain communication

New operations can repair damaged parts of the inner ear.

Perforated eardrum

(d) What is a perforated eardrum?

Swimming is not advised when an eardrum is perforated.

(e) List some ways in which an eardrum can become perforated.

Key ideas summary
This revision procedure can be done as a quick check at any time.

Sound is created by a _____ object. A drum skin or a triangle are examples of this. Sound has to travel through a _____ to the ears where it vibrates the eardrum, which marks the boundary between the _____ ear and the _____ ear. Vibrations are converted into electrical impulses in the _____ which is part of the _____ ear.

Sound waves that are close together have a _____ pitch. Where the waves are far apart the pitch is _____. If the waves have a high _____ the sound is loud. Where the waves have a low _____ the sound is quiet.

14 The Earth and beyond

Space is really big

14.1 Galaxies and stars
(a) Put these features in order of size and give a brief description of each.

* sun
* Earth
* white giant star
* universe
* galaxy
* red dwarf

Stars have a finite life. They change from a stable star, like our sun at the moment, to other forms.

Our neighbours

(b) We live in the Milky Way. True or false? Explain.

(c) We live in the Andromeda galaxy. True or false? Explain.

Children are fascinated by the size of things and where we live. They love writing their full galactic address.

(d) Our nearest star is Proxima Centauri. True or false? Explain.

Galaxies

(e) All galaxies are spiral spinning discs of stars. True or false?

The number of stars

(f) Which is the right answer? Our local galaxy contains:
- more than 100 billion stars
- more than 100 million stars
- more than 1 million stars
- too many stars to count

14.2 The solar system

The planets

(a) Name the planets in order from the sun outwards.

Size of planets

(b) List the planets in order of size.

Invent your own way of remembering the order.

(c) List the rocky planets.

Oxygen-rich planets

(d) List the planets with an oxygen-rich atmosphere.

14.3 The moon and eclipses

(a) Why can we see the moon?

(b) Why does the moon appear to change shape?

Remember to think about whether the lit up part of the moon is on the right or the left as you look at it.

(c)

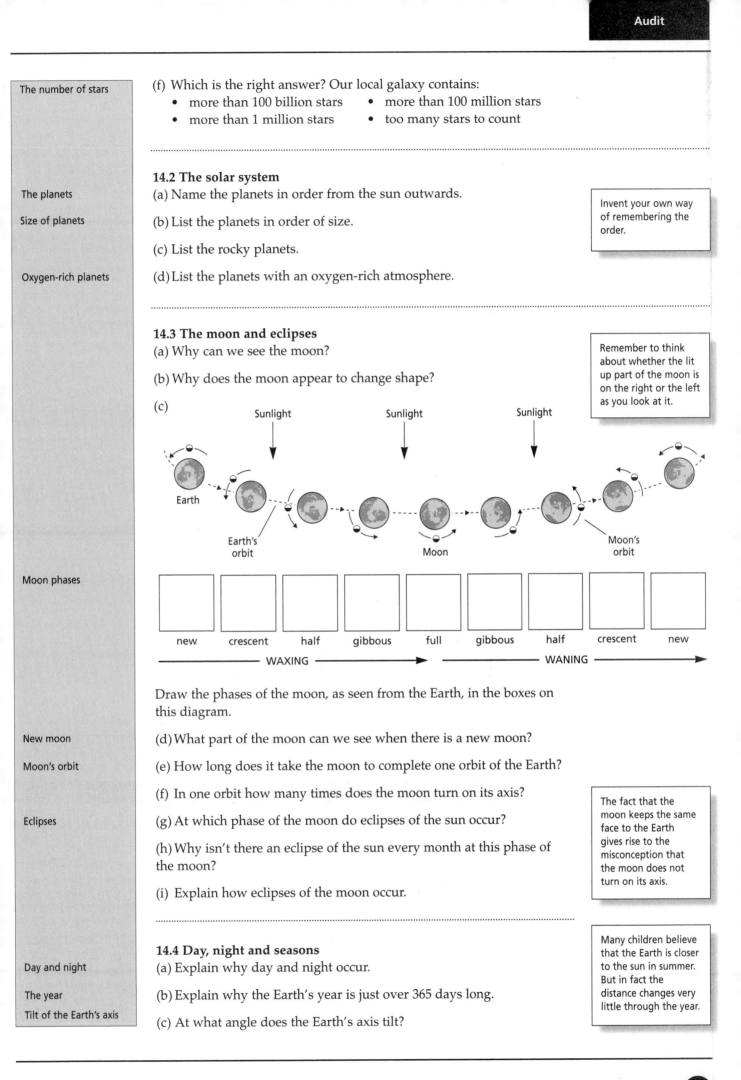

Moon phases

Draw the phases of the moon, as seen from the Earth, in the boxes on this diagram.

New moon

(d) What part of the moon can we see when there is a new moon?

Moon's orbit

(e) How long does it take the moon to complete one orbit of the Earth?

(f) In one orbit how many times does the moon turn on its axis?

Eclipses

(g) At which phase of the moon do eclipses of the sun occur?

The fact that the moon keeps the same face to the Earth gives rise to the misconception that the moon does not turn on its axis.

(h) Why isn't there an eclipse of the sun every month at this phase of the moon?

(i) Explain how eclipses of the moon occur.

14.4 Day, night and seasons

Day and night

(a) Explain why day and night occur.

The year

(b) Explain why the Earth's year is just over 365 days long.

Tilt of the Earth's axis

(c) At what angle does the Earth's axis tilt?

Many children believe that the Earth is closer to the sun in summer. But in fact the distance changes very little through the year.

(d)

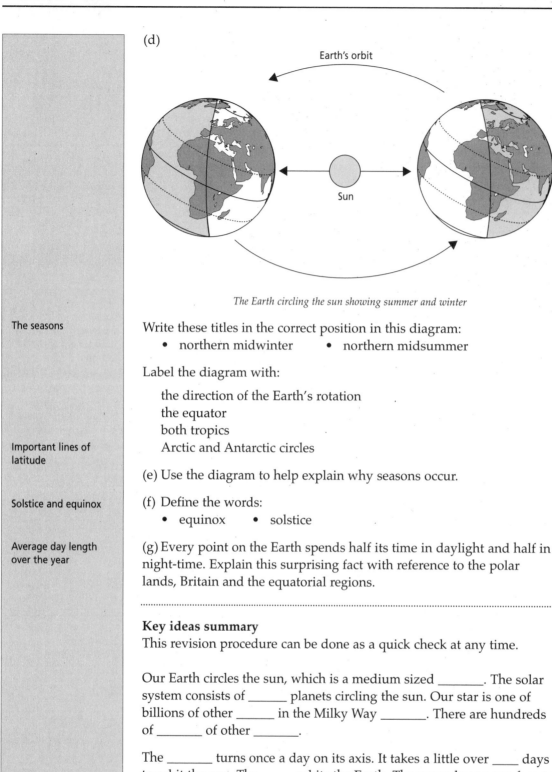

The Earth circling the sun showing summer and winter

Write these titles in the correct position in this diagram:
- northern midwinter
- northern midsummer

Label the diagram with:

the direction of the Earth's rotation
the equator
both tropics
Arctic and Antarctic circles

(e) Use the diagram to help explain why seasons occur.

(f) Define the words:
- equinox
- solstice

(g) Every point on the Earth spends half its time in daylight and half in night-time. Explain this surprising fact with reference to the polar lands, Britain and the equatorial regions.

Key ideas summary
This revision procedure can be done as a quick check at any time.

Our Earth circles the sun, which is a medium sized _____. The solar system consists of _____ planets circling the sun. Our star is one of billions of other _____ in the Milky Way _____. There are hundreds of _____ of other _____.

The _____ turns once a day on its axis. It takes a little over _____ days to orbit the sun. The _____ orbits the Earth. The moon keeps one face to us which means it must complete ___ turn each month on its axis. The moon is ____ when it is on the opposite side of the Earth to the sun. The moon is ____ when it is between the sun and the Earth. _____ happen only rarely because the _____ orbit is tilted in relation to the Earth's orbit round the ____.

Feedback

Early theories of
disease

Food preservation

1.1 How science works
(a) Before germ theory people believed that disease was caught from
bad air or was the result of displeasing God.

(b) Before Pasteur people believed that substances contained the agents
of their own decay. Pasteur's experiments suggested that if you kill
yeasts and bacteria in a foodstuff by heat then prevent airborne
microbes from reaching it, it will stay fresh for an extended period.

> Think about what
> happens after you
> unseal the lid of a jar
> of jam.

1.2 Evidence informs and shapes theory
(a) The sort of questions you might have asked would have depended
on your temperament but they might have included: What is the
recovery rate of your patients? Does it hurt? What does it cost? On
what theory do you base this treatment?

> Perhaps medieval
> doctors were very
> persuasive.

Flat Earth

(b) People in medieval Europe believed the evidence of their senses.
Much of what was easily observable of the motions of the sun, moon
and planets would have seemed to support a flat-Earth theory.

However, the ancient Greeks already knew the Earth to be spherical
because, for example, the masts of boats appear on the horizon before
their hulls do and at any single moment in time the position of the sun
as seen from the ground varies according to the observer's viewpoint.

> By 300 BC Greek
> mathematicians had
> calculated the
> diameter of the Earth
> with great accuracy.

(c) The circumnavigation of the globe by Magellan and Cook, and more
recently pictures taken from space, make this indisputable.

1.3 Science cannot explain everything
The creation of the
universe

(a) Any evidence, if there was any, would have been completely
overlain by subsequent events. Also, it could be argued that time itself
started at the beginning of the universe, so the question 'what came
before' may make no sense at all.

> Questions which begin
> with 'What' are
> relatively easy. 'Why'
> questions are much
> more tricky.

Predicting the future

(b) Weather systems are too complex to be predicted many days
ahead. However, the effects of large-scale changes are becoming better
understood. For instance, the effects of El Niño are now largely predictable.

(c) The interaction between genetics and the environment is too
complex for any predictions to be made until scientists have all possible
information.

1.4 Ethical considerations

Disease genes

(a) People who carry increased risk based on their genes may be disadvantaged, for example by being refused health and life insurance. Also, some people simply do not want to know when they will die.

> This is already a concern with some types of breast cancer.

(b) Answers will vary. You might want to know because this would inform decisions about whether you have children or about financial planning for the future. On the other hand, you may take the view that everyone dies eventually and no one knows when they are going to die.

The environment

(c) Brent Spar was a huge platform in the North Sea which was to be sunk in deep ocean water. This plan was abandoned after protests and concern about pollution. Arguments against dumping included the risk of toxic chemicals finding their way into the ocean and contaminating fishing grounds, and that an amount of steel as large as this should be recycled. An argument in favour was that it would be vastly more expensive and energy consuming to bring the platform ashore and recycle the material. In the end, the claims of Greenpeace in this case were seen to be based on some false assumptions, and many scientists believe sea dumping would have been better.

> Scientists cannot simply report their findings because in many cases the findings are so complex they need interpretation.

Immunization risks

(d) There will be many possible answers to this. All informed opinion says that except for a few susceptible children everyone should be immunized. This is because the risk from the disease far outweighs the risk involved in immunization. Some doctors suggest that emotional and uninformed parents should not be told of the risks since they may take an irrational decision.

> Everyone knows the health risks from cigarettes yet a substantial minority of people still smoke.

Parents may say that they will be the ones who have to live with their choice so they should be given all available information and be trusted to make sensible choices.

Key ideas summary

Science is a way of looking at the world that relies on evidence from observations. These observations are not made at random, they are guided by theories. Science progresses when existing theories no longer explain what we see. When this happens scientists devise new theories which are tested against the available evidence. Most scientific ideas change over time as new evidence and new ways of interpreting it come to prominence.

In one view of science, often referred to as the classic view, scientists must first decide on the idea/theory/area they want to investigate. They try to collect all the evidence concerning that area of science. They then attempt a working hypothesis (see page 46) and test it by experiment. The hypothesis and the evidence are published. Other scientists test it by conducting experiments of their own. If just one of these refutes the original hypothesis then a new hypothesis is needed. Sometimes theory outstrips experimentation. In the case of Einstein's theory of relativity the confirmatory experiments could only be conducted years after the original idea was put forward.

The pursuit of science poses ethical (moral) questions. Should scientists alarm the general population by telling them about a real but marginal health risk, for instance? Should scientists take a stand on issues such as experimentation on human foetuses, test tube pregnancies for older women, and human cloning?

2 Scientific investigations

Deciding on questions which will make good practical investigations

2.1 Not all questions can be investigated practically

(a) These could be answered practically in the classroom:

How far do cars roll off a ramp? Let toy cars roll off a ramp.

Do most people prefer chocolate ice cream to vanilla? Survey a sample of pupils in the class.

How fast does sound travel? Have a partner stand as far away as possible on the school field. Clap two pieces of wood together. Notice how long after the wood has been clapped together that the sound is heard.

These present practical problems:

Why do I like chocolate ice cream? Impractical because it is too complex and subjective.

How fast does electricity travel? Impractical in primary classrooms because the equipment to measure it is too expensive, but it is practical to do this in laboratories.

What will the weather be like tomorrow? Impractical because weather systems are highly complex, but can be done fairly accurately with sophisticated computers.

Do you get food poisoning if you eat raw chicken? Impractical because of ethical and safety considerations.

Questions about growth

2.2 Constructing questions which can be investigated

(a) There are many possible questions. The following questions can all be investigated by experiments. They are characterized by the words 'What happens if … ?'. They invite comparison of one set of conditions with another.

> These questions can be investigated at home or in school.

Do the beans sprout best in the dark? (Put some in the dark and others in the light and see which germinate best. Keep all other conditions identical.)

What are the best beans to use? (Try three sorts of bean. Give each variety a score for factors such as ease of sprouting, amount of sprouts and taste. The one with most points is best.)

What is the best temperature for sprouting beans?

Do the beans sprout best when they are really wet?

Do the beans sprout best when they are in big jam jars?

How much water do you need to give them?

Do the beans sprout best if the top is covered with a cloth?

Are your questions 'What happens if …' questions? Do they invite comparison of the outcomes?

Measuring dependent variables

(b) In each of the experiments you want to find the 'best' way to sprout beans. 'Best' can be defined in a number of ways: quality, size, the speed of sprouting of the bean sprouts. In this case the quality and size of the sprouts are the dependent variables.

> Changes in the dependent variable are not directly under the experimenter's control.

(c) There are many questions. Here are some suggestions:

Which bird is seen most often?
Which bird stays longest?
What sort of food do the birds like to eat?
Do the same kinds of birds visit every day?
Do the birds feed in the same places?
Is it one individual bird which visits more than once or are there several different birds of the same kind?

Notice that none of these questions starts with 'why'. 'Why' questions are often difficult to investigate.

Hypothesizing and guessing

(d) *guess:* to express an uninformed, haphazard opinion which is formed without detailed calculation.

predict: to forecast based on previous experience.

hypothesize: to make a prediction based on previous experience and scientific knowledge.

(e) These sentences have been completed using the words above.

I *hypothesize* that the weight will fall faster than the ball because the weight is heavier than the ball and I think that all heavy things fall faster than lighter ones.

I *guess* that the weight will fall faster than the ball, but I've never thought about it before.

I *predict* that the weight will fall faster than the ball, based on what I've seen before.

I *hypothesize* that the red car will travel faster than the blue one because its wheels are smoother and I think smooth wheels cut down friction.

I *guess* that the red car will go faster than the blue one.

I *predict* that the blue car will beat the red because it did last time.

> An hypothesis is like a prediction with a 'because' statement on the end.

(f) Also ask your colleague to assess the quality of your work on this.

2.3 Planning investigations and controlling variables

Investigating heat insulation

(a) Equipment needed:

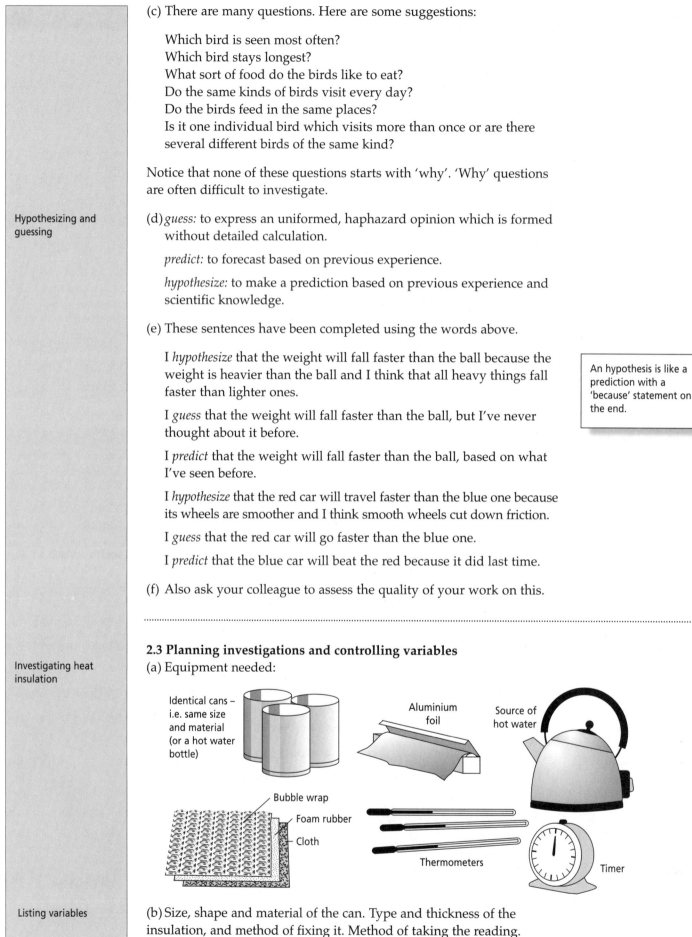

Identical cans – i.e. same size and material (or a hot water bottle)

Aluminium foil

Source of hot water

Bubble wrap
Foam rubber
Cloth

Thermometers

Timer

Listing variables

(b) Size, shape and material of the can. Type and thickness of the insulation, and method of fixing it. Method of taking the reading. Timing of the temperature readings.

(c) Time, type of insulation, and thickness of insulation would all be independent variables. We could alter each one systematically. Temperature is the main dependent variable which we would measure.

Time and temperature are also continuous variables (see section 2.10).

Reliability

(d) Reliable results are those which can be trusted. They are the outcome of a well-designed experiment.

To make the results reliable you would need to make sure that all the variables were controlled, i.e. kept as near as possible the same. The one variable you would alter would be the type of insulation.

Graphing results

(e) In the form of a line graph with time along the horizontal axis and temperature on the vertical axis. Each type of material would have a separate line. Lines could be shown in different colours.

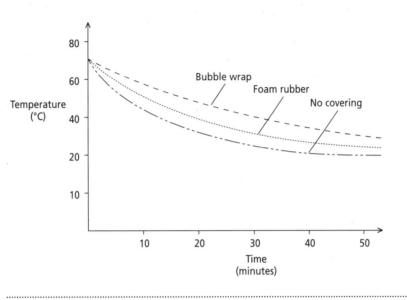

2.4 Selecting samples and interpreting data

Measuring the heights in a class

(a) *Girls are taller than boys.* The data does not give information about girls and boys in general. It only refers to this class, which may not be representative.

Children may sometimes want to generalize too much from a simple restricted test.

On average girls are taller than boys. The data does not give information about girls and boys in general.

Jane is taller than Jim. (Both are in the class.) The data supports this.

In this class, on average, girls are taller than boys. The data supports this.

Girls are taller than boys because they mature earlier. The data supports the first part of this statement but it cannot tell us **why** the situation is like this.

Most girls are taller than most boys. This data does not give information about girls and boys in general.

Sampling bird visits

(b) After break the type of bird seen most often was the pigeon. Of the birds we saw the wren was seen least often. The total number of visits by birds was 70. Four types of birds were seen.

Avoid trying to stretch data too far.

Note that the data provides no evidence to allow claims to be made about the behaviour of the birds.

Scattergram

2.5 The reasons for anomalous results

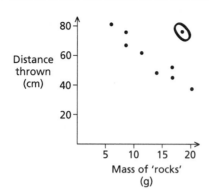

Distance thrown (cm) / Mass of 'rocks' (g)

Graphs make it much easier to see results which do not fit the general pattern.

Anomalous results

(a) The odd, or anomalous, one is circled. It is clearly a fluke or mistake as all the other readings are grouped together. In general if one reading is completely distinct from the others it is likely to be incorrect.

(b) The arm of the catapult might have been pulled back further or the weight might have been in a different position on the throwing arm. The weighing of the projectile might have been done incorrectly.

(c) They drew the graph well and accurately. Can they see one result which doesn't fit the pattern? What do they want to do about the result? (Probably best to ignore/discount it.) Extend the work by asking the children to interpret the graph, report the trend and try to quantify their result.

2.6 Interpreting outcomes in the light of scientific evidence

Making sense of the observations

(a) You will need to know a number of things about electricity and materials or be able to work them out from the evidence of the experiment. These include:

the brightness of bulbs depends on the current flowing through them
pencil lead is made from carbon (graphite) mixed with clay
pencil lead is a resistor
the longer a piece of carbon the more it resists the flow of electricity.

A pencil lead resistor dims a bulb.

(b) Pencil lead, in spite of its name, is not a metal. We might be able to work this out because all metals are good conductors of electricity. Pencil lead is not a metal but one of the few non-metals which conduct electricity.

(c) A living room light dimmer relies on a length of carbon through which the electricity flows. The greater the length of carbon the more the electricity is resisted.

There are many instances where the results of experiments both confirm existing knowledge and increase our knowledge.

2.7 Collecting evidence

Ecological investigation

(a) You could peg out a line, moving away from the trunk. Every 50 cm along the line you could place a small hoop and make a note of the species found in each hoop. This technique is a form of sampling; it would be impossible to check every single plant so you simply note plants in the hoops. (50 cm is an example: a different measurement could be used.)

Sampling is a technique used in all ecological investigations.

Measuring very tall objects

(b) You could stand at a distance from the tree and find the angle between your line of sight and the top of the tree using a protractor. Then you could use trigonometry to calculate the height.

Maths and science are interdependent in this instance.

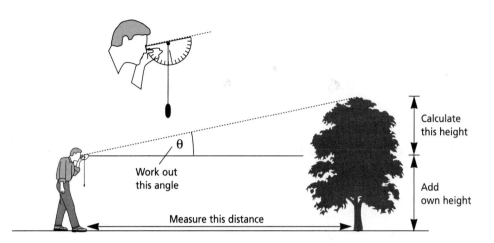

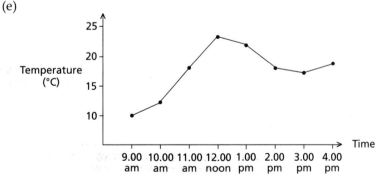

Alternatively you could stand a person next to the tree, then estimate, from a distance, how many times that person would need to be stacked up to reach the top of the tree.

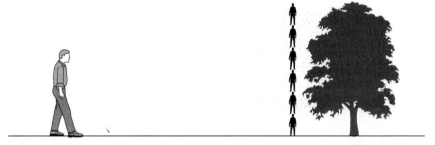

(c) No, you would expect the results to vary. However, most of the results are likely to cluster around a central value, with only a few being very slow or very quick. The trend should be easy to see.

This is an easy investigation to try out now. Ask a helper to hold a ruler vertically by its tip just above your open hand, then to let it go. Note the ruler reading at the point where you catch it. Do this ten times.

You will probably notice that the marks you get for essays show the same sort of pattern.

Bar charts

(d) The bar chart would have a cluster towards the centre of the graph around the most common/average height. The most common value is called the **mode**. It is a type of **average**. The middle value of a series is called the **median**.

(e)

Line graphs

Temperature (°C)

25

20

15

10

9.00 am 10.00 am 11.00 am 12.00 noon 1.00 pm 2.00 pm 3.00 pm 4.00 pm

Time

(f) There are several possible interpretations but it is quite likely that:

it was summer time
the sky was clear between 9am and 1pm
clouds came over between 1pm and 2pm
the day stayed cloudy between 2pm and 4pm.

Alternatively:

> the thermometer was on a wall which was sunny in the morning
> and in shadow after midday.

(g) The dependent variable is temperature. The independent variable is
time.

Continuous variables

(h) A continuous variable is one which has an infinite number of points
on a scale. Continuous variables include length, weight, mass, speed
and musical pitch.

Line graphs can only be used to record continuous variables.

Statistics

(i) Newcomers to statistics should find the following titles a useful
starting point: Rowntree, D., *Statistics without Tears*; and Pentz, M. and
Stott, M., *Handling Experimental Data*.

2.8 Measuring and validity

(a) *reproducibility:* refers to whether an experiment can be done by
different people and still obtain similar results.

Valid and reliable

validity: refers to whether the techniques used in an investigation are
sound and the experimenter has measured what should have been
measured. For example, have all the variables been controlled?

reliability: is concerned with whether the results of an experiment fall
within the same range each time the experiment is repeated.

(b) Reproducibility

> *The scientist found that no one else got the same results when they tried
> her experiment.*

> *The class teachers got one result when administering the spelling test but
> the head got another.*

Validity

> *No one trusted the results because the experiment did not control variables.*

> *The teacher gave the children different maths tests and then tried to rank the
> children in order of ability.*

Reliability

> *The scientist found that his experiment gave different results every time he
> tried it.*

> Use these examples to
> help you remember.

Accurate measurement

(c) You should use the smallest possible container (ideally 30 ml in this
case). You must look for the meniscus, which is where the surface of the
water curves as it touches the side of the container. You must put the
container on a level surface.

Parallax error

(d) Parallax error occurs when you take readings at an angle to the scale
on a measuring instrument. Try this with a ruler. If you look directly
at the scale you get the true reading, but if you look at an angle you
get an incorrect reading. This effect is particularly pronounced with
thermometers since the scale is some way from the alcohol.

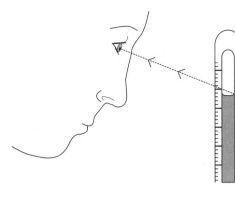

When we read a thermometer at an angle, our eye sees an alignment between the liquid and a point on the scale.

Distorted by parallax, this is not a true reading of the liquid level.

Parallax error when reading a thermometer

2.9 Units of measurement

SI (Système Internationale) units are used throughout the world by scientists.

Abbreviation	Unit	What it measures	Measuring instrument	Notes
N	newton	force	force meter (spring balance)	See pages 88–9.
kg	kilogram	mass	balance	See pages 90–91.
J	joule	energy	force meter (for instance)	See pages 88–9.
W	watt	power	ammeter and voltmeter	
A	amp	current flow	ammeter	
V	volt	electrical energy	voltmeter	
Ω	ohm	resistance	voltmeter and ammeter	See page 83 for information about measuring electricity.
°C	Celsius	temperature	thermometer	
ml	millilitre	volume	measuring jug or cylinder	Use cm³ as an alternative.
dB	decibel	sound level	sound meter	

Other sections of the *Feedback* have further information about the units detailed here.

2.10 Graphs and charts

Growth chart

(a) The day is the independent variable (the experimenter decides when to take the measurement) and the height is the dependent variable. Independent variables are capable of being altered systematically by the experimenter. For instance, if you wanted to find out if sugar dissolved more quickly in hot water than in cold, you could systematically alter the temperature of the water.

See section 2.7 for more on line graphs.

Independent and dependent variables

The dependent variable changes in response to changes in the independent variable. In the case of the dissolving sugar the speed of dissolving is the dependent variable.

(b)

x and *y* graph axes

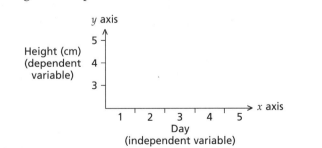

This is a good example. You can apply the same principles widely.

The day is on the horizontal (*x* axis); independent variables are always placed on this axis. The height goes on the vertical (*y* axis); dependent variables are always placed on this axis.

(c) A bar chart is used commonly in primary schools. Its *x* axis can represent individual items such as different balls.

A histogram is not the same as a bar chart.

A histogram is more complex. The width of the bars depends on the class intervals which may not always be the same size. The area of each bar of a histogram needs to be taken into account.

Line graph opportunities

(d) *the number of swings made by a pendulum each minute* ✓ The length of the string (continuous variable) is on the *x* axis.

the distance a ball is thrown by different people ✗ The *x* axis would have individual people on it and these are discrete variables. Variables are discrete when there are no values between items. For instance layers of insulation are discrete; you cannot have one and a half layers.

the colour of eyes of pupils in the class ✗ The pupils are discrete variables.

(e)

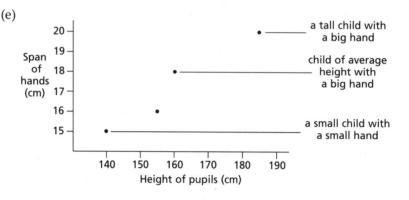

Scattergram

Opportunities for scattergrams

(f) There are many investigations which could be recorded on scattergrams. In general these are instances where you suspect that there is a relationship between two values but there could be some variation in the relationship. As one of the values gets bigger so does the other. This is true of all the investigations listed below:

the weight and height of people
the engine size and top speed of cars
the amount of watering and the growth of plants.

Scattergrams are done quickly and easily by computers. They use numbers entered in a spreadsheet. See the companion volume, *Teaching Science in Primary Schools*, for more on the use of spreadsheets.

(g) Line graphs could be constructed if your investigation involves two continuous variables. Some examples are given below (the independent variable is given first in each instance):

the time and the temperature of a cooling tin
the height (in cm) of a ramp and the distance travelled by a car rolling off it
the area of a parachute and the time taken to fall
the weight put in the toe of a stocking and the stretch which results.

If you have any doubt about whether your suggestion could be made into a line graph, try sketching it out.

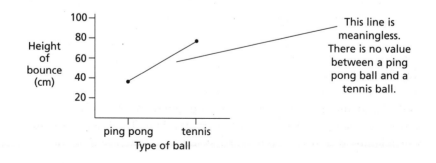

Sketching ideas for graphs is a quick way of checking whether a graph is possible.

2.11 Keys

(a) There are a number of ways in which a key could be constructed. Here is an example with a binary sorting mechanism.

A key showing the vertebrates

		ALL VERTEBRATES		
Scales and gills	Smooth skin Lays eggs in water	Scales Lays eggs on land	Feathers	Hair Feeds young Milk
FISH	**AMPHIBIANS**	**REPTILES**	**BIRDS**	**MAMMALS**

There are five groups of vertebrates:
fish
amphibians
reptiles
birds
mammals.

Binary keys rely on yes/no answers at decision points. Others rely on giving several options at the decision point.

Binary key

(b)

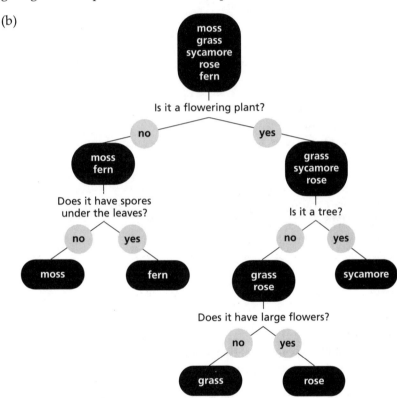

This is a binary key. It is also called a 'dichotomous' or branching key. A dichotomous key branches into two possible choices.

(c) Multiple choice keys are common in identification books:

    A sycamore   B pine   C holly   D fir   E laurel

(d) A good key will have unambiguous questions and offer clear choices.

(e) *The Clue Book* (Allen, G. and Denslow, J., Oxford University Press) is a classic series with some of the easiest-to-follow keys. Look for the six titles which have been reissued in revised editions (1997).

Learn how to use the key types yourself then teach the children how to use them.

Leaf key

Construct your own key.

Use a published key.

....

Key ideas summary

When conducting investigations scientists need to know ways to control and **change** variables. The **independent** variable is the one which we change systematically. The **dependent** variable is the value which changes in response to changes in the **independent** variable.

Continuous variables include values such as **temperature, length** and **weight**. On the other hand values like number of bricks or number of insulation layers are examples of **discrete** variables.

Scientific investigations do not always yield expected or consistent results. This may be because of poor design, incorrect **measurement** or simply because there was no pattern there to discover. We should also look back at the **original** question when trying to interpret the results of any investigation.

3 Health and safety requirements

Asthma problems

3.1 Health, safety and the Law
(a) The lizard would be safer to keep since the guinea pig's fur might cause an allergic reaction in the child. However, you should think very carefully about keeping any animal in the classroom for more than a few days.

(b) Apart from the young of *Homo sapiens* (the human being) there are no really suitable mammals for the classroom. Gerbils sleep most of the time, mice smell and guinea pigs will make enough noise and fluff to disturb most classes.

Legal constraints

(c) Grass snakes, newts and frogs, in common with all native reptiles and amphibians, are protected species and there are hefty fines if you disturb them. However, it is legal to collect a small number of frog's eggs from a private or school pond. You should release them at the back leg stage.

(d) Terrapins can carry very virulent bacterial infections.

> Rare and endangered creatures are protected by law and you cannot legally collect them, even from your own pond.

3.2 Burning
(a) In the infant classroom there should be one adult to each table during any activity involving burning.

Safety with candles

(b) In the upper junior classroom there should be: minimum paper on the desk; restricted movement around the room; hair and clothes tied back; no one out of their seat; stable candle holders; sand trays or non-flammable bases. Make sure fire extinguishing equipment (e.g. a wet cloth) is available. However, do not feel this is a very hazardous undertaking. With reasonable precautions the lesson will be successful and safe.

Burning fabrics

(c) Ensure there is adequate ventilation when burning fabrics, or do it outside. Use very small threads of fabric or pieces smaller than a fingernail. Remember that some synthetics emit toxic fumes.

> Smoke detectors might be a problem when doing this.

(d) *Be Safe* is a valuable guide published by the Association for Science Education (ASE, College Lane, Hatfield, AL10 9AA).

Safety at the seaside

(e) A rocky seashore is very hazardous. Prepare the pupils and make sure they know the rules. Complete a risk assessment first. Ensure children have adequate footwear and the sort of bags that allow their hands to be free. Check the times of the tides and set very strict limits to the freedom of movement for the children. Keep as a group as far as

possible. Have a ratio of children to teachers of less than 10 : 1. Have a first-aid kit available.

(f) Any cuts (other than minor scrapes), any head injuries, broken bones and any limb sprains which do not clear up within a few minutes.

4 Functions of organisms

Life processes

4.1 All living things show seven life processes

(a) All living things perform the life processes of:

See section 4.8 on photosynthesis.

nutrition	Animals eat plants or other animals. Plants make food (sugar) in their leaves using the process of photosynthesis.
movement	All animals move; even barnacles which are stuck to rocks move their bodies. Plants' leaves and flowers follow the sun.
growth	Most animals stop getting bigger when fully grown, but they carry on repairing their bodies; an example is skin growing over a cut. Most plants carry on getting bigger all their lives.
reproduction	All living things die eventually but they leave behind young so that their species continues.
respiration	Food provides energy. Animals and plants break down food using oxygen. They produce carbon dioxide as a waste product.
excretion	Living things produce waste. They have to get rid of it from their bodies or it will poison them. Animals produce ammonia which is so poisonous that it is turned into the less poisonous substance urine.
sensitivity	Animals use senses like touch and sight. Plants are also sensitive and can respond to light and gravity. Some, like *Mimosa pudica* (the sensitive plant), respond to touch.

Plant life processes

(b) Children find it difficult to see that plants move, feed or excrete.

The movement of plants is slow and is the result of the influence of light (phototropism) or gravity (geotropism). Plants make their own food through photosynthesis, but this process is unlike the way in which animals feed. Plants break down this food during the process of respiration.

Is it alive?

(c) Yes, they are alive. Seeds are dormant until water or light conditions trigger germination. Cut flowers are alive since each individual cell is still carrying on life processes.

Is fire alive?

(d) Fires move, they consume fuel, they use oxygen, they excrete carbon dioxide and they seem to reproduce themselves.

Children often have misconceptions about this. You may find it difficult to convince them of the life of seeds and cut flowers.

However, they are not sensitive, they do not have a cellular structure and do not respond to stimulus. We would need to discuss with children that fires do not actually reproduce themselves in the same way as living things.

Human life processes

Seven indicators of life

Coma

Death

Human gut

Functions of parts of
the gut

4.2 Life processes in humans

(a) We know that people are living things because they show all the
seven signs of life. They:

feed	People are omnivores; they eat food from both plants and animals.
move	People move on two legs. Most paralysed people can still move their eyes.
grow	They stop growing in size at about 18 years, but can grow new skin at any age.
reproduce	Women can produce babies within their reproductive life-span. Men can father children into their old age.
use energy	You can tell that people are alive and using energy because they breathe.
excrete	People excrete used food in their solid faeces. They excrete liquid as urine and sweat.
are sensitive	Their five senses are: sight, hearing, touch, smell and taste.

(b) A person in a coma still exhibits evidence of all the life processes.
These include the ability to reproduce, as was shown when a woman
was successfully artificially inseminated with sperm taken from her
husband when he was in a coma.

(c) Death is diagnosed when all brain activity stops. Older children may
find a debate about the care of coma victims thought-provoking.

Humans show the
same life processes as
all other animals.

Production of carbon
dioxide is a by-product
of respiration.

Find out about the
problems associated
with diagnosing
persistent vegetative
state.

4.3 The specialized functions of the human gut

(a) The correct order is:

1 mouth	3 stomach	5 large intestine
2 oesophagus	4 small intestine	6 anus

(b)

The alimentary canal

Stomach acid is
stronger than battery
acid.

(c) *removal of the water from food waste* happens in the *large intestine.*
absorption of soluble food into the blood happens in the *small intestine.*
mixing of food with strong acid is done in the *stomach.*
chopping of food into small pieces happens in the *mouth.*
carrying the food into the stomach is done by the *oesophagus.*

Food passes through
the gut wall into
the blood. Food is
dissolved in the blood
for distribution to the
rest of the body.

4.4 Human circulation

The function of the heart

(a) This stylized drawing might not resemble the heart very closely, but drawings like this are a valuable tool in assessing the extent to which the person doing the drawing understands the function being represented.

The heart has four chambers.

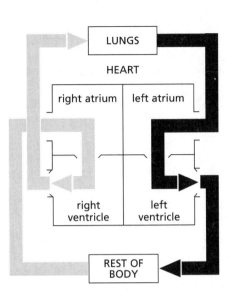

Stylized diagram of the circulatory system

The heart is a muscle which pumps blood around the body. It is divided into two halves. One half pumps blood to the lungs. The other half pumps blood to the rest of the body.

Each half of the heart has two chambers.

The function of the blood vessels

(b) The three types of blood vessel are:

arteries which have thick muscular walls and take blood under pressure from the heart.

veins which are smaller in diameter than arteries and have a thin muscular wall. They have valves which stop the blood flowing the wrong way. They carry blood back to the heart.

capillaries which are very small blood vessels with walls so thin that materials such as oxygen, carbon dioxide and glucose can pass through them.

A cut artery will squirt blood. A cut vein will ooze blood rapidly.

(c) Oxygenated blood normally travels away from the heart in arteries.

Pulmonary circulation

(d) The one exception is the pulmonary vein which takes oxygenated blood from the capillaries in the lungs to the heart.

Pulmonary is an adjective meaning 'connected with the lungs'.

Red and blue blood

(e) Deoxygenated blood is blue but the moment it oozes out of your body it comes into contact with the air and becomes red, the colour of oxygenated blood.

Haemoglobin plus oxygen is red.

Pulse rate

(f) Exercise causes the pulse rate to increase. It can sometimes be difficult to locate your pulse points, and slightly chubby children find this almost impossible. There are a number of instruments which will measure pulse rate.

Many children will not connect the pulse with the heart beat unless this is taught directly.

(g) The blood carries the two things which cells need to respire: oxygen, and energy in the form of glucose. When muscles are exercising they need to respire (get energy from food) more quickly than when resting.

The function of blood

(h) The functions of parts of the blood are:

platelets help with blood clotting.

haemoglobin is a substance which combines with oxygen; it is contained in red blood cells.

phagocytes are the white blood cells which engulf bacteria and viruses thereby protecting the body from attack.

plasma is the clear liquid which is left when the blood cells have been removed. It is the fluid within which the other components are carried.

lymphocytes are white blood cells which produce antibodies to help fight disease.

(i)

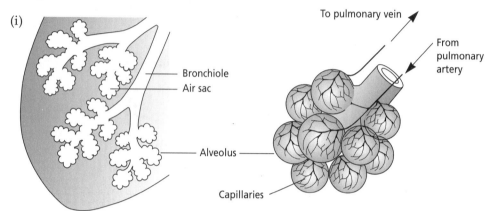

Part of a lung and its blood supply

The lungs and gas exchange

Gas exchange happens in the lungs. There is a dense network of airways with a supply of *capillaries*. The air is supplied from the mouth through the windpipe (*bronchus*). This branches into a large number of smaller tubes called *bronchioles*. There are small bag-like structures at the end of each bronchiole called *alveoli* which have a network of capillaries. *Oxygen* is absorbed into the blood and *carbon dioxide* is passed out of the blood through the capillary walls.

> Inhaled air consists of 78% nitrogen, 21% oxygen and 0.03% carbon dioxide. Breathed-out air contains about 5% carbon dioxide.

Transport to the cells

(j) Blood also carries food to the cells of the body. This is in the form of dissolved sugars, amino acids and fatty acids which can be used readily by the cells.

Waste removal

(k) Blood carries away waste products. Carbon dioxide is one. Others include urea and mineral salts.

(l) The idea of blood carrying oxygen is often easiest for children to understand. Many children would not think it possible for food to be dissolved so that it can be carried in blood.

4.5 Human movement

Skeleton

(a) See facing page for a labelled diagram of the human skeleton.

Bones

(b) The names of bones that children at Key Stage 1 might know include knee bone, shin bone, skull, spine, ribs, hip bone and jaw bone.

> The old song 'Your knee bone's connected to your shin bone ...' is fun and instructive.

(c) Key Stage 2 children might know the scientific name 'humerus' (the upper arm bone) since it is the funny bone.

> Elvis shook his pelvis.

Joints

(d) *ball and socket joints:* hip, shoulder.
hinge joints: knee, elbow.
sliding joints: between the vertebrae of the backbone and between the small bones of the ankles and wrists.

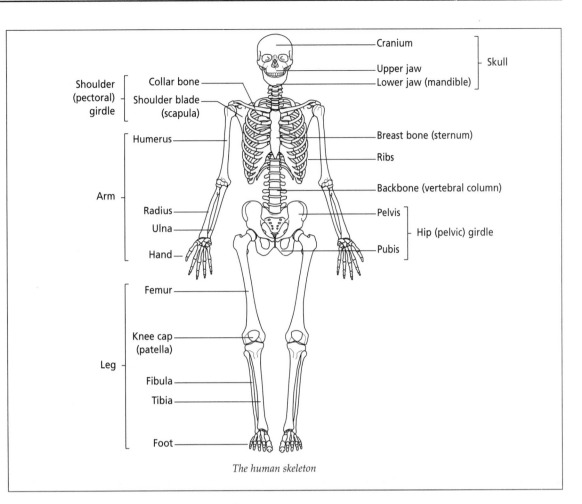

The human skeleton

(e) The forearm will bend upwards at the elbow.

(f) Antagonistic muscles are pairs of muscles which work on the same joint but in opposite directions. The biceps and triceps are a pair of antagonistic muscles in the upper arm. The front thigh muscle pulls the leg straight and the back thigh muscle bends the leg at the knee.

'Antagonists' in all walks of life pull away from each other.

(g)

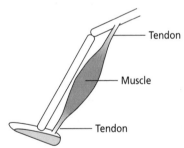

Muscle attachment

Muscles are attached to bones by tendons, which are bands of tough connective tissue. Tendons are sometimes confused with ligaments which strap bones together at a joint.

Check that you can distinguish between:
ligaments
tendons
cartilage.

(h) There are several ways to show this. A simple way is shown here.

The rubber band acts like a bicep pulling the forearm upwards.

4.6 Human reproduction and growth

Reproduction parts

(a) *testes:* the organs which produce sperm.

ovaries: the organs which produce ova (unfertilized egg cells).

fallopian tubes: these allow eggs to pass from the ovaries to the uterus.

uterus: the Latin name for the organ commonly called 'womb' where foetuses develop.

placenta: the organ which supplies the foetus with nutrition and oxygen and removes waste products.

sperm: the male reproductive cells.

embryo: the stage after fertilization until two months.

foetus: a human embryo changes into a foetus at about two months.

> Look for any similarities in terms to do with reproduction in plants and animals.

What is an organ?

(b) The organs are testes, ovaries, uterus, placenta.

(c) Any explanation would have to be checked against the school's sex education policy.

In vitro fertilization

An egg is removed from the ovary (a woman's egg producing organ). Sperm which has been donated by a man is placed in a glass test tube with the egg. A sperm cell fuses with the egg to fertilize the egg. This embryo is allowed to grow in the test tube to the size of a tiny full stop. It is then placed in the woman's womb to develop naturally.

4.7 Plant roots and stems

Roots

(a) A root:

anchors the plant
draws up water
absorbs dissolved salts.

> Roots produce tiny root hairs which can be seen under the microscope.

Tubers

(b) Potatoes sprout shoots. Only stems can do this, which means that potatoes must be swollen underground stems and not roots at all. Swollen roots include carrots and radishes.

Bulbs

(c) Daffodil bulbs and onions are swollen leaves. Chop them open to see the compressed leaves with the shoot in the middle. Roots cannot produce shoots.

4.8 Leaves and photosynthesis

Photosynthesis

(a) Photosynthesis is the production of simple sugar using the pigment chlorophyll in a plant leaf. Carbon dioxide and water are combined using the energy of sunlight.

> Glucose is a simple sugar. Sucrose and starches are closely related to this simple sugar.

Simple chemical equation

(b) $6CO_2 + 6H_2O \rightarrow C_6H_{12}O_6 + 6O_2$.

(c) No. Animals do not contain chlorophyll.

Plant food

(d) Fertilizer is often referred to as plant food. You can buy bottles of it labelled as such.

Good soil with high levels of fertilizer promotes growth. Plants need chemicals from the soil in order to make important compounds such as proteins. Glucose, made by photosynthesis, provides other raw materials and energy for this.

Respiration in plants

(e) This process is respiration. Both plants and animals break down sugar to produce energy. This breakdown releases carbon dioxide.

> Both plants and animals respire.

Plants and animals produce carbon dioxide all the time.

During the day plants produce more oxygen than they use, but during the night they cannot photosynthesize so their production of oxygen is nil.

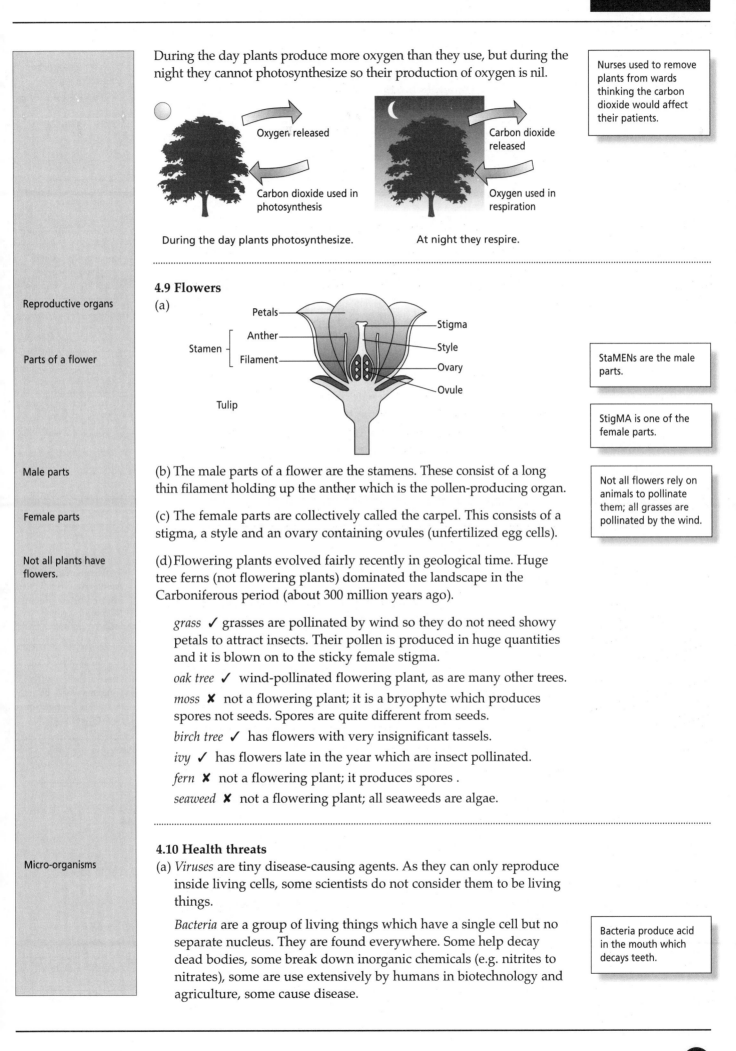

Oxygen released

Carbon dioxide used in photosynthesis

During the day plants photosynthesize.

Carbon dioxide released

Oxygen used in respiration

At night they respire.

Nurses used to remove plants from wards thinking the carbon dioxide would affect their patients.

4.9 Flowers

(a)

Petals
Anther
Stamen
Filament

Stigma
Style
Ovary
Ovule

Tulip

Reproductive organs

Parts of a flower

StaMENs are the male parts.

StigMA is one of the female parts.

Male parts

(b) The male parts of a flower are the stamens. These consist of a long thin filament holding up the anther which is the pollen-producing organ.

Female parts

(c) The female parts are collectively called the carpel. This consists of a stigma, a style and an ovary containing ovules (unfertilized egg cells).

Not all flowers rely on animals to pollinate them; all grasses are pollinated by the wind.

Not all plants have flowers.

(d) Flowering plants evolved fairly recently in geological time. Huge tree ferns (not flowering plants) dominated the landscape in the Carboniferous period (about 300 million years ago).

grass ✓ grasses are pollinated by wind so they do not need showy petals to attract insects. Their pollen is produced in huge quantities and it is blown on to the sticky female stigma.

oak tree ✓ wind-pollinated flowering plant, as are many other trees.

moss ✗ not a flowering plant; it is a bryophyte which produces spores not seeds. Spores are quite different from seeds.

birch tree ✓ has flowers with very insignificant tassels.

ivy ✓ has flowers late in the year which are insect pollinated.

fern ✗ not a flowering plant; it produces spores .

seaweed ✗ not a flowering plant; all seaweeds are algae.

4.10 Health threats

Micro-organisms

(a) *Viruses* are tiny disease-causing agents. As they can only reproduce inside living cells, some scientists do not consider them to be living things.

Bacteria are a group of living things which have a single cell but no separate nucleus. They are found everywhere. Some help decay dead bodies, some break down inorganic chemicals (e.g. nitrites to nitrates), some are use extensively by humans in biotechnology and agriculture, some cause disease.

Bacteria produce acid in the mouth which decays teeth.

Fungi are living things which many scientists regard as being separate from plants. They share many plant characteristics but do not produce chlorophyll. They feed on dead or living organisms and some are agents of disease and decay.

See section 4.8 on photosynthesis.

Infective agents

(b) *Viruses* can infect humans with diseases such as smallpox, measles, mumps, yellow fever, polio, flu and colds, HIV, warts.

Bacteria cause gangrene, septic wounds, ear infections, leprosy and food poisoning.

Fungi cause athlete's foot, thrush and ringworm.

Parasites

(c) Mosquitoes transmit a tiny single-celled parasite called *Plasmodium*, which is a microscopic protozoan. This parasite can live in both humans and mosquitoes. It causes symptoms of fever in humans and can lead to death. Similar diseases are transmitted by blood-sucking tsetse flies which inject *Trypanosoma*. In humans these cause sleeping sickness.

Single-celled animals are called protozoa, which are the simplest first animals.

4.11 Healthy animals and plants

Body defences

(a) White blood cells attack and engulf any foreign bodies which enter the bloodstream. Antibodies bind on to bacteria and viruses to make them harmless. Blood platelets clot to form a crust to stop any other bacteria or viruses entering the body.

See the functions of the parts of the blood in section 4.4 (h).

Immunity

(b) Immunizations and vaccinations work by introducing weakened or dead viruses or bacteria (see above) into the body. The body then produces antibodies which recognize the virus or bacterium. After this, if infective material of the same type enters the body, antibodies are produced rapidly to destroy it.

Grooming behaviour

(c) Birds and mammals spend a large amount of time grooming to remove parasites such as fleas and ticks from their fur or feathers.

People used to be infected by lice, hence the phrase 'feeling lousy'.

Parasite removal

(d) There are many possible answers to this. The following is only a selection.

Cattle in tropical countries are visited by egrets which pick off insects from their backs. Large fish allow cleaner wrass or other fish to eat skin parasites from them.

These are examples of symbiosis where both organisms benefit from each other's presence.

Birds have dust baths to get rid of ticks. Cattle and rhino roll in the mud to form a protective layer over their skin.

4.12 Drugs and people

HIV

(a) HIV infection is associated with sharing of needles in intravenous drug use during which blood from one person becomes mixed with the blood of another through injection.

Tobacco

(b) Tobacco smoke contains nicotine and tar.

Nicotine is a drug to which people get addicted. Addicts feel they need regular doses of tobacco smoke. Tar is a sticky substance which clogs up smokers' lungs. The lungs of a smoker produce a great deal of mucus which makes it difficult for some smokers to breathe. Tar also contains chemicals which cause lung cancer (carcinogens).

It seems that scare tactics do little good in preventing children from smoking.

Health warnings

The babies of women who smoke are more likely to be small and die early. Breathing other people's cigarette smoke is also dangerous.

(c) Smoking causes fatal diseases.
Smoking causes lung cancer.
Smoking causes heart disease.
Smoking when pregnant harms your baby.
Protect children: Don't make them breathe your smoke.

Medicines

(d) *Antibiotics* can treat some bacterial infections, e.g. septic cuts, venereal diseases and encephalitis.
Antihistamines can treat allergies such as hay fever.
Fungicides can treat fungus disease such as thrush.
Aspirin can treat mild pain and mild arthritis.

4.13 Healthy people

Types of food

(a) proteins – meat, fish, nuts and beans.
fats – oil, butter, nuts and cheese.
carbohydrates – sugar, bread, rice and pasta.

Vitamins

(b) Vitamins are chemicals, small amounts of which are vital to life. Since the body cannot make most of them (an exception being vitamin D which is made by the skin in sunlight), vitamins are obtained through eating a varied and healthy diet.

> People in rich countries have expensive urine. Most people's diets already have enough vitamins. Excess vitamins taken as vitamin pills are excreted.

Disability and health

(c) Good health is not the absence of disease since few people are completely disease-free. A person in a wheelchair can be healthy but disabled. A person suffering from asthma or poor eyesight or hearing problems may also feel perfectly well and in good health. Health is a feeling of well-being as experienced by an individual.

Mental health

(d) Depression is a feeling of great dejection and hopelessness. Schizophrenia is characterized by delusions and paranoia. Anxiety is suffered by people who feel unaccountably worried by experience which the majority of people cope with easily. Other mental illnesses include phobias, compulsive habits, hypochondria and mental breakdown.

> Mental illness is caused by a combination of life events and inherited susceptibility.

(e) The largest number of prescriptions is for mental illness.

4.14 Cells are us

Single cells

(a) Most cells can be seen only with a *microscope*. To see them you need to get a very thin slice of tissue and shine light through the slice. Typical cells in your body are about 20 thousandths of a millimetre across.

> The first cells known to science were cork bark cells drawn by Robert Hooke in 1665.

(b) Single-celled organisms include bacteria, protozoa such as amoeba, and some algae.

Plant and animal cells

(c) Plant cells have a cell wall made of cellulose surrounding each individual cell. Woody plants in addition deposit a material called lignin around each cell. Heartwood consists of dead hollow cells encased in lignin.

> Plant cells are tough and much more robust than animal cells.

Many plant cells also contain chloroplasts in which the green chemical chlorophyll is found.

63

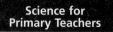

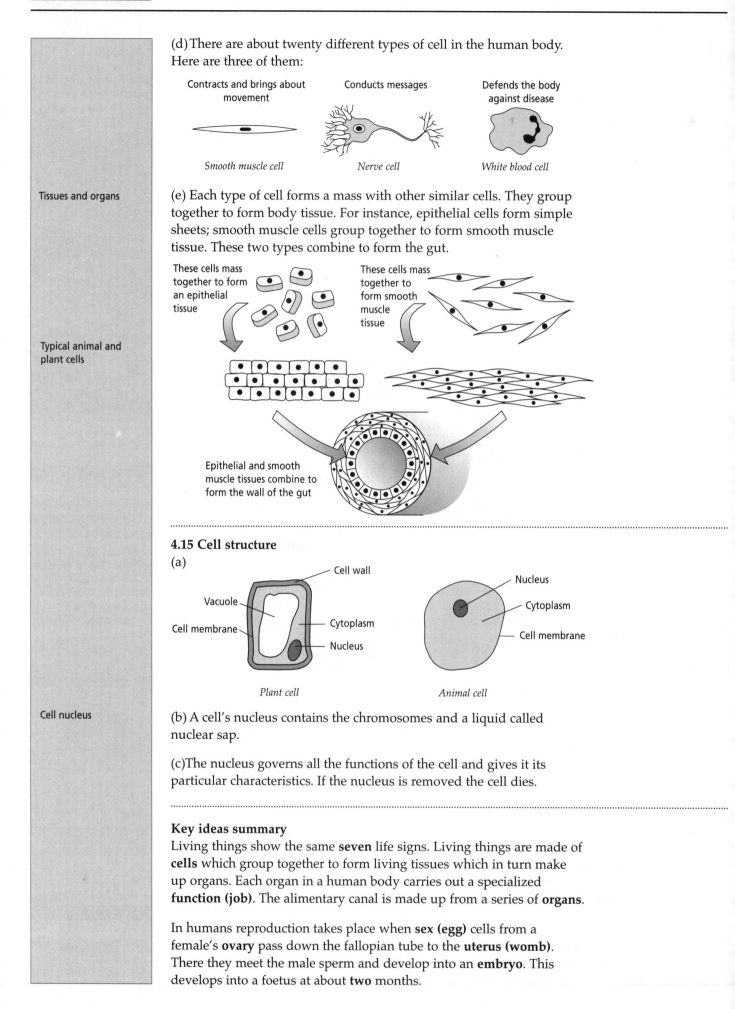

Tissues and organs

Typical animal and plant cells

Cell nucleus

(d) There are about twenty different types of cell in the human body. Here are three of them:

Contracts and brings about movement

Conducts messages

Defends the body against disease

Smooth muscle cell   *Nerve cell*   *White blood cell*

(e) Each type of cell forms a mass with other similar cells. They group together to form body tissue. For instance, epithelial cells form simple sheets; smooth muscle cells group together to form smooth muscle tissue. These two types combine to form the gut.

These cells mass together to form an epithelial tissue

These cells mass together to form smooth muscle tissue

Epithelial and smooth muscle tissues combine to form the wall of the gut

4.15 Cell structure

(a)

Cell wall

Vacuole

Cell membrane

Cytoplasm

Nucleus

Plant cell

Nucleus

Cytoplasm

Cell membrane

Animal cell

(b) A cell's nucleus contains the chromosomes and a liquid called nuclear sap.

(c) The nucleus governs all the functions of the cell and gives it its particular characteristics. If the nucleus is removed the cell dies.

Key ideas summary
Living things show the same **seven** life signs. Living things are made of **cells** which group together to form living tissues which in turn make up organs. Each organ in a human body carries out a specialized **function (job)**. The alimentary canal is made up from a series of **organs**.

In humans reproduction takes place when **sex (egg)** cells from a female's **ovary** pass down the fallopian tube to the **uterus (womb)**. There they meet the male sperm and develop into an **embryo**. This develops into a foetus at about **two** months.

Plants use the energy in sunlight to combine **carbon dioxide** and **water** to give **glucose**. This sugar is the plants' food. Plants use **leaves** to trap the sun's light to power the chemical reaction of **photosynthesis**. Roots are the parts of plants which anchor the plant and draw up water and **nutrients (chemicals).** Plants, in the same way as animals, respire when they break down **sugars (food)** to power their life processes. Flowering plants reproduce when the female egg cell is **fertilized** by the male pollen cell.

Human health is affected by a number of factors including **genetic** and environmental influences. Tobacco is one environmental factor which has a major effect on health. Micro-organisms including bacteria, **viruses**, protozoa and **fungi** have health implications for people. Vaccination works against **viruses**, such as flu and polio, by alerting the body to produce **antibodies** against any subsequent invasion. Antibiotics do not kill viruses and fungi – they are only effective against **bacteria** such as those causing meningitis or syphilis.

Cells comprise a **nucleus** and other materials enclosed in a cell **membrane**. Cell nuclei contain **chromosomes** which are made up from a series of genes, many of which programme the body to develop in different ways. All this **genetic** material is made from **DNA**. This is a complex molecule which can replicate itself during cell division. Plant cells are much more robust than **animal** cells because they are surrounded by a tough **cellulose** wall. Plant cells also contain **chloroplasts** which take part in photosynthesis.

5 Continuity and change

5.1 Life cycles and reproduction

Does he look like his dad?

(a) The organisms which are born looking like miniature versions of their parents include all mammals except the spiny anteater and the platypus which, unusually for mammals, lay eggs. The pouched mammals of Australia give birth to foetuses which crawl into the pouch to complete their development into juveniles.

All other vertebrates hatch from their eggs looking like their parents.

Insect clones

Some insects such as greenfly are born as identical clones of their mothers. Other insects, such as dragonflies, have a nymph stage which looks very similar to the parent.

Free-swimming larvae

Many invertebrates such as corals, which are sedentary as adults, hatch from eggs and go through a free-swimming stage. At this point they do not look like their parents. Most insects have a larval stage which does not resemble the parent.

Insect life cycle words

(b) *larva:* the stage which hatches from the egg; it is usually worm-like and unlike the adult.

> *pupa:* the resting stage in a hard case between larva and adult when the larva undergoes metamorphosis.

> *cocoon:* the hard case in which the pupa metamorphoses.

> *metamorphosis:* the process of change between larva and adult.

> *caterpillar:* the larva of a butterfly or moth.

Not all insects go through complete metamorphosis; see below.

maggot: the larva of a fly or beetle.

chrysalis: the pupa of a butterfly or moth.

nymph: the larval stage in insects which have no pupal stage, e.g. the dragonfly; nymphs are larvae which look like their parents. Compare this with the caterpillar stage of moths and butterflies.

(c) Insects have complex life cycles which may or may not involve a pupal stage.

Insects with a pupal stage which involves complete metamorphosis include bees, wasps, ants, houseflies and butterflies. In all these insects the larvae look unlike the adult. The insect undergoes metamorphosis in the pupal case.

| Caterpillars are the larvae of moths and butterflies. They have six jointed legs, just like the adult form. |

Two different types of insect life cycles

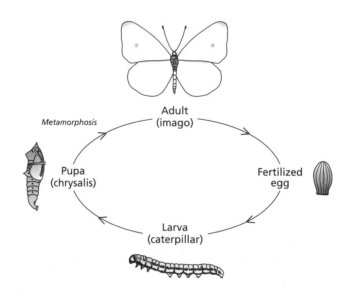

Life cycle of the butterfly

Insects without a pupal stage

Another group of insects have no pupal stage. Their larvae (nymphs) resemble the adult. This group includes dragonflies, locusts, grasshoppers and termites. In all these insects the larval stages resemble the adults but are not the same.

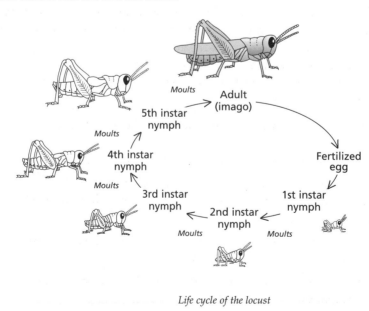

Life cycle of the locust

Seed producers

(d) ✓ cactus   seaweed   moss   mushroom
    ✓ pine tree   fern   ✓ dandelion

> Only flowering plants produce seed.

Seeds are always the result of sexual reproduction in which parts of two individuals fuse to become one.

Asexual reproduction

(e) Most other plants, such as mosses, algae and ferns, reproduce asexually by means of spores. Fungi also reproduce using spores; the mushroom cap is merely a spore-producing body. Fungi, ferns, algae and mosses can all reproduce sexually if conditions are harsh. This leads to the production of individuals with a variety of new characteristics which may be better suited to survival.

> See section 6.1(h) for information about how closely fungi and plants are related.

Vegetative reproduction

Plants can also reproduce vegetatively. This happens when part of a root, leaf or stem is cut off and planted. Each piece then forms a new plant.

> Vegetative reproduction is a form of cloning. The exact DNA of one individual is reproduced.

5.2 Genes in cells

(a) Starting with the smallest element:

Genetic material

genes are the parts of a chromosome which determine particular characteristics. Each gene is made up from DNA.

> The human genome project is mapping the location of each gene on the human chromosome.

Chromosomes

*chromosome*s are the long structures inside each cell nucleus composed of many genes.

nucleus is the structure which contains the chromosomes.

cell is the structure which contains the nucleus.

> People with Downs Syndrome have one extra chromosome.

(b) Every cell (except the sperm or egg cells) in your body has a set of 23 pairs of identical chromosomes (46 in all).

Egg and sperm cells

(c) Egg or sperm cells have only 23 single chromosomes. When the egg and sperm cells fuse the resulting cell has the full complement of 46 chromosomes. This means that the new individual has characteristics from both parents.

> Chimps share over 95% of their genetic information with humans, but they have a different number of chromosomes.

5.3 Genetics and reproduction

Clone

(a) Dolly is a clone. A clone is an individual whose DNA, genes and chromosomes (all its genetic material) are identical to its parent.

> Identical twins are clones of each other apart from their fingerprints and iris patterns, both of which are unique.

Dolly the sheep was grown using a single cell from her mother's breast. Further cells were developed in the laboratory then implanted back into her mother's womb. Dolly then grew naturally. She is the first large animal to be cloned using artificial techniques. She is physically identical to her mother. In fact, her mother is actually her mother and her father in some senses.

(b) *dominant gene:* in any pair of chromosomes there are two genes for every characteristic. If the two genes are dissimilar then one will be expressed in the characteristic; this is the dominant gene.

recessive gene: this is the gene which is not expressed as the characteristic when the partner gene on the other chromosome is dominant.

homozygous: where both genes for the same characteristic on the different chromosomes are identical.

heterozygous: where the genes for the same characteristic on the different chromosomes are different.

Genes

(c) Our appearance is determined by the genes we inherit from our parents. Genes are made up from DNA. Each parent contributes half the full complement of chromosomes (which are made up from many genes). We do not look identical to either parent but neither are we simply an average of both of them. Where a gene is dominant, that gene will be expressed in our appearance whilst the complementary recessive gene from the other parent is not expressed.

Dominant and
recessive characteristics

(d) The *RR person* will roll her tongue because she is homozygous for rolling. The *rr person* will not roll her tongue because she is homozygous for not rolling. The *Rr person* will roll her tongue because she is heterozygous with rolling dominant.

Eye colour

(e) All the children will have blue eyes if both parents are blue eyed.

b = blue (recessive)   B = brown (dominant)

father bb ——————— mother bb

baby bb   baby bb   baby bb   baby bb

father Bb ——————— mother bb

baby Bb   baby Bb   baby bb   baby bb
(brown)   (brown)   (blue)   (blue)

Inherited diseases

(f) Both parents have to have a copy of the gene for sickle cell anaemia or cystic fibrosis for the child to get the disease. The gene is recessive so neither parent shows the disease. However, there is a one in four chance that each child will inherit a recessive gene from both parents. If this happens the child will have the disease.

(g) In the sperm cell and the egg cell the chromosomes do not make copies of themselves. In each sperm and egg cell there are 23 single chromosomes. They will find their partner when the sperm and egg fuse.

Intelligence

(h) Most psychologists believe that intelligence is a combination of unalterable genetics and the conditions in which children are brought up. So a child with a genetic predisposition to high intelligence reared in a stimulating environment is highly likely to be intelligent. A child with poor genetic inheritance reared in the same environment will never be as intelligent as the first child but will be able to function well.

Identical twins

(i) Identical twins (those sharing identical DNA) separated at birth are ideal subjects for investigation in this respect. Separation of this sort tends to happen during war years when there is considerable turmoil, although it rarely happens in the west today. The evidence about inherited and acquired intelligence in identical twins is based on very respectable data not tainted by Nazi associations. The data produced by Cyril Burt (an eminent psychologist) on this subject was flawed by cheating but there is a mass of good data from studies on twins today.

5.4 Evolution

Inherited or acquired?

(a) *The ability to speak English* is an acquired characteristic and cannot be inherited.
A big nose can be inherited.
A disease like haemophilia can be inherited.
A disease like polio cannot be inherited.

Possible factors in children's backgrounds such as broken families and uncertain paternity mean that there are many issues about whether work on this topic can be done in the classroom.

This style of working out possible gene combinations is useful in many instances.

A *single* copy of the sickle cell gene has the beneficial side-effect of conferring some protection against malaria.

This is a highly contentious area but one which teachers should discuss openly.

In the early nineteenth century Lamarck believed that many acquired characteristics could be inherited.

Only those characteristics which are determined by our genes can be inherited.

Darwin

(b) *On the Origin of Species* (1859).

(c) The theory of evolution by natural selection: those individuals of the same species which are best equipped to survive will be the ones to breed and thus pass on their genes to the next generation.

Backbones evolved only once.

(d) All vertebrates have a backbone. In each type of fish, amphibian, reptile, bird and mammal this backbone has a very similar pattern. It is highly unlikely that such a complex and intricate system developed more than once and this strongly suggests that all vertebrates are descended from a common ancestor.

> Classification (see section 6) is based largely on evidence of the evolutionary history of the animal and plant groups.

(e) The human appendix indicates that our ancestor was a plant-eater able to digest cellulose. Its presence has little or no bearing on whether or not we breed so it is still passed on to the next generation.

(f) Many vertebrate embryos share common characteristics at early stages in their development; humans, fish and chickens are very alike in the first weeks after conception. This suggests that vertebrates may have a common ancestor.

> The study of the development of individuals is called *ontogeny*.

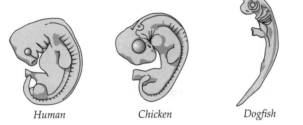

Human   *Chicken*   *Dogfish*

Galapagos finches

(g) Darwin thought that a few finches had been blown to the isolated birdless islands. Those with long thin beaks prospered by eating insects and those with strong beaks did well at seed crushing. The finches which had particularly long beaks or strong beaks prospered to a greater extent than their average brothers and sisters. Over thousands of years these traits were selected. The insect-eating finches and the seed-eating finches gradually evolved characteristics which made them markedly different in type both from each other and from their common ancestor.

> To become a new species animals have to become isolated geographically, behaviourally and/or in appearance.

Fossils

(h) *Archaeopteryx* is a fossil which looks very like a small dinosaur with feathers. It is definitely a bird (because it has feathers) but is clearly closely related to dinosaurs. Modern birds have evolved to look less like dinosaurs than *Archaeopteryx*. It is an animal which is halfway between two groups of animals and is the best example of this evolutionary state in the fossil record.

> The study of fossils is *palaeontology* – the study of ancient life.

5.5 Species

What is a species?

(a) A species is a group of living things which can breed and have fertile offspring. Humans could physically mate with gorillas but no progeny would ensue.

Hybrids

(b) Horses can breed with donkeys to produce mules but mules cannot breed as they are sterile.

Human hybrids?

(c) Humans and chimps cannot be hybridized since the number of chromosomes each has is not identical. Humans have 23 pairs and chimps have 24 pairs of chromosomes.

Key ideas summary

All living things go through **stages (changes)** in their lives. Even humans which are born looking very like adults go through a great many changes before sexual **maturity**. Most animals hatch from externally laid **eggs**. Many insects have a complex life **cycle** which involves stages such as egg, **larva (caterpillar)** and **pupa**. Corals and other sedentary animals have a **larval** stage which can swim freely leading to new colonies.

Evolution occurs when the inevitable mistakes in DNA copying (mutation) lead to the occasional advantageous **change (mutation)**. The environment favours living things which are best equipped to exploit the available **food (space/niche)**. Even a small **advantage** over an otherwise similar animal of the same species can lead to an individual's survival and ability to pass on **genes** to the next generation.

Sickle cell anaemia and cystic fibrosis are examples of **inherited** diseases. Parents can be **carriers** of the disease gene but be unaware of this because the gene is **recessive** and they are heterozygous for the gene. Only if an adult has children by a similar **heterozygous** carrier may their children be **homozygous** for that gene and therefore have the disease.

6 Ecosystems and classification

6.1 The classification of organisms

Classifying vertebrates

(a) Fish, amphibians, reptiles, birds and mammals.

(b) *Fish:* scaly skin, gills, live in water. Cold blooded.
Amphibians: soft moist skin, lay eggs in water. Cold blooded.
Reptiles: dry scaly skin, lay eggs in leathery cases on land. Cold blooded.
Birds: feathers, lay eggs in hard shells. Warm blooded.
Mammals: hair, give birth to live young, feed them on milk. Warm blooded.

Arthropods

(c) Arthropods are all the small invertebrates with jointed legs (arthro = joint, pod = leg).

(d) Insects. Even the caterpillars of insects have six true legs; the stubby things at the back of the caterpillar are not true jointed legs.

Eight-legged arthropods

(e) Spiders and scorpions.

(f) Crustaceans (e.g. woodlice and crabs) and myriapods (e.g. centipedes and millipedes).

(g) Sea urchins and starfish (the echinoids).

(h) Fungi cannot make their own food by photosynthesis. They can only feed on organic material.

(i) A lichen is a mixture of algae and fungus. (The algae makes the food and the fungus traps the moisture.)

(j)

cow, man, <u>trout</u>	the others are mammals
<u>ostrich</u>, tortoise, snake	the others are reptiles
seahorse, shark, <u>lizard</u>	the others are fish
<u>spider</u>, butterfly, grasshopper	the others are insects
crab, woodlouse, <u>scorpion</u>	the others are crustaceans (the scorpion is more like a spider)
toadstool, <u>moss</u>, dry rot	the others are fungi

6.2 Ecology words

(a) *habitat:* the place where a particular organism can survive. Under a rotting log is a good habitat for woodlice.

ecosystem: a community of living organisms with its physical environment, containing producers, consumers and decomposers. A forest is an example of an ecosystem.

adaptation: the ways in which an animal or plant is changed to suit its environment. A fish is adapted to water by means of its gills and streamlined shape.

ecology: the study of relationships between plants, animals and their environment. You can study the relationship between the shade of a tree and the plants which can grow beneath it.

environment: the conditions in which an organism lives. Some seaweeds live in an environment which is dried out then submerged under water several times a day.

(b) Woodlice, centipedes, spiders, millipedes, ivy, lichen, moss, fungi and ants are among the plants and animals which may live here. Fungi will be able to feed on the decaying material.

(c) Fungi, moss, algae, lichen, greenfly, caterpillars, maggots, wasps, blue tits, blackbirds, squirrels and hawks.

(d) Answers will vary. Discuss them with colleagues.

(e) Predator or carnivore
Producer
Consumer or herbivore
Consumers

(f) The total amount of energy in an ecosystem depends largely on the amount of sunlight available to it. Plants must have sufficient water and carbon dioxide to convert the sunlight into vegetation. This material is used by grazing animals to make their bodies. Predators use the food energy in the bodies of their victims to make their own bodies. Energy is used up through the food chain so there is little left over for predators at the top of the chain. If there is little green vegetation at the

Science for Primary Teachers

start of a food chain then it is most unlikely that there will be enough energy to support any big, dangerous predators.

(g) Plants produce the oxygen that animals need. Plants produce all the food that animals need. Plants remove carbon dioxide (a waste product from animals) from the atmosphere.

(h) The only habitats with no connection to green plants are:

the deep ocean vents. Bacteria eat the sulphide-rich, boiling-hot water coming out of the volcanic holes in the Pacific Ocean.

deep in the rocks of the Earth's crust. The existence of bacteria here has only been recently confirmed but some scientists think that these organisms represent a huge biomass which may be responsible for some of the Earth's gas and oil deposits.

hot water geysers where heat-loving bacteria thrive in temperatures over 110°C. They live on the chemicals exuded in the volcanic water.

> These two environments were not suspected 50 years ago.

6.3 Types of micro-organisms

(a) There are many examples of each. Here are a few:

viruses: HIV, polio, measles, cold, flu.
bacteria: Listeria, E. coli, cholera and syphilis-causing bacteria.
protozoa: Amoeba, Euglena, Trypanosoma, Plasmodium.
fungi: Penicillium, Candida, potato blight, mildew, plant rust, yeast (brewing and baking).

Compost

(b) Fungi and bacteria.

Sewage

(c) Most bacteria respire just like animals and plants. Most produce carbon dioxide and water. The water from sewage farms can be pure enough to enter water treatment works and then be used for drinking water.

> Micro-organisms are essential to human survival. Only a tiny minority are harmful.

6.4 Humans affect their environment

Sulphur burning affects the environment.

(a) Sulphur plus oxygen gives sulphur dioxide. Sulphur dioxide plus water gives sulphurous acid. This is a main ingredient of acid rain.

Acid rain can also be made when natural carbon dioxide dissolves in water to make carbonic acid.

> Acid rain is natural in some circumstances.

Acid rain

(b) Acid rain can make lakes too acid for fish life. It can make soil too acid for tree growth. Acid rain can also kill the foliage of living trees.

The effects of acid rain can be reproduced in the classroom by diluting vinegar and watering seedlings with different concentrations of this solution.

The greenhouse effect

(c) Gases in the atmosphere trap heat which is being radiated by the Earth. If the gases of the Earth's atmosphere did not trap heat the Earth would be at about −15°C, which is far too cold for life. The main greenhouse gases are carbon dioxide, water vapour, ozone and methane. Human industry is emitting large quantities of carbon dioxide, so increasing the layer of gases, which is enhancing the effect.

> The physics of the greenhouse effect are clear but the causes and effects are hotly disputed.

(d) It may cause the Earth to warm up, which could result in the melting of the ice caps and huge changes to the climate.

Ozone

(e) Ozone is a type of oxygen which is formed by three atoms of oxygen instead of the usual two.

> The depletion of the ozone layer and the enhanced greenhouse effect have different causes and different effects.

The ozone layer	(f) Ozone gas is found between the stratosphere and the ionosphere. It absorbs harmful ultraviolet rays from the sun and prevents them from reaching the surface of the Earth. In this context, ozone is good for all living things. At lower levels in the atmosphere ozone is produced by engines and is a toxic part of the smog associated with bright sunlight in big cities such as Los Angeles and Mexico City.
The hole in the ozone layer	(g) Refrigerant gases such as CFCs destroy the ozone layer in a highly complex series of chemical reactions. If the ozone layer is destroyed, ultraviolet light will cause skin cancer and eyesight problems in humans and disrupt the photosynthesis of plants.

See section 12, Light, for information on ultraviolet.

Key ideas summary

There is a huge variety of living things in the world. There are at least 40 million different **species**. They are divided into groups which are based on their **evolutionary** history. For instance, sharks and dolphins are not considered to be closely **related** even though at first sight they look **similar**. Sharks and dolphins have quite distinct evolutionary histories with sharks being related to other **fish** and dolphins being **mammals**.

Food chains show which animals feed on which plants and animals. All food chains, except those round deep **ocean** vents and deep inside the rocks of the continents, start with a **green** plant.

The greenhouse effect is vital to life on the planet. However, the enhanced greenhouse effect caused by industry may create changes which will bring dramatic **climate** changes. The depletion of the ozone layer is caused by chemicals released by people. These **combine** (react) with ozone in the **upper** atmosphere allowing more **ultraviolet (UV)** light to reach the Earth's surface.

7 Particle theory

7.1 Particles

Particle size	(a) 1 electron 2 atomic nucleus 3 atom 4 molecule
Atom	(b) Atoms are far too small to be seen with even the most powerful microscope. An atom is the smallest part of an element. An atom has all the chemical properties of the element, and atoms of the same element have the same properties (if you could see them they would be identical to each other). Atoms take part in chemical reactions.
Atomic structure	(c) This is a diagram of a hydrogen atom. It has only one proton and one electron. All other elements are more complex. The next most complex atom, helium, has two protons and two neutrons in the nucleus which is circled by two electrons.

Since atoms are so small how do we know they exist? (See section 1, The nature of science.)

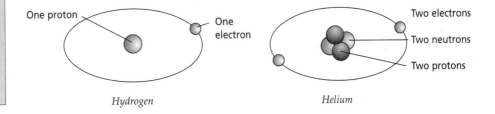

One proton   One electron   Two electrons
                                          Two neutrons
                                          Two protons

Hydrogen   *Helium*

73

Electron

(d) An electron is a particle which orbits the nucleus. Electrons have a negative charge. Metals have free electrons which move between atoms, and this is important to understanding why metals conduct electricity.

Use this knowledge in section 9.1, Conductors and insulators.

Ion

(e) An ion is a charged particle. It is an atom, or group of atoms, which has lost or gained an electron. If the atom has lost an electron it becomes positive, if it has gained an electron it has a negative charge.

Salt crystals are made from ions of chlorine and sodium.

(f) No. Even very fine particles ground up physically will contain many atoms and molecules.

7.2 Chemical bonding

Bonding

(a) There are two main types of chemical bond. These are electrovalent (also called ionic) and covalent bonds.

When atoms join together they try to form the most stable arrangement. In the case of sodium and chlorine the sodium transfers one electron to the chlorine. The resulting chlorine ion is negatively charged and the sodium is positively charged. The two unlike charges attract each other very strongly. This is electrovalent bonding.

In the case of hydrogen and carbon the atoms share electrons to make a stable compound. This is covalent bonding.

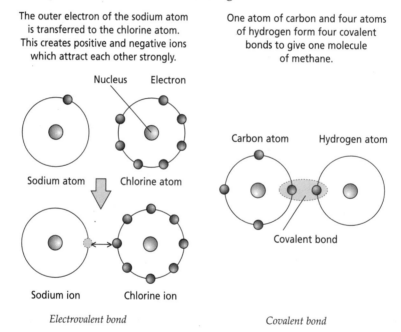

Electrovalent bond   *Covalent bond*

Glucose

(b) $C_6H_{12}O_6$. This means that each glucose molecule is made from six atoms of carbon, twelve atoms of hydrogen and six atoms of oxygen.

See section 8.2 (j) for information on how glucose is broken down.

Starch

(c) The digestion has to break apart the long chains (called polymers) of starch before it can digest the simple sugar (glucose).

Fats

(d) Fats are made from hydrogen, carbon and oxygen (yes, that's the same as glucose). However, they are bonded in a much more complex way than sugars or starches. They require longer digestion.

Fats are chemically very complex but are made of the same elements as sugars.

Fats typically have a molecule of glycerol linked to three molecules of fatty acid.

Energy drinks

Dense energy

(e) Athletes drink a solution containing glucose because it takes less time for the energy to become available to the body.

(f) Polar explorers eat a great deal of fat and relatively little pasta because fats contain a lot energy in a dense form. This density reflects their complex chemical bonding. Pasta contains energy but in a far less dense form. A little fat gives the same calories as a lot of pasta or bread (starch).

Glucose drinks really do what the adverts suggest (but they are just sugary water).

Key ideas summary
All **matter (material)** is made up from atoms. Atoms consist of a large number of particles that include **protons** and neutrons which form the nucleus and **electrons** which orbit the nucleus. An **ion** is a charged particle which has lost or gained an electron. **Atoms** bond together to form molecules.

Elements are made up from one sort of atom. **Compounds** are made up from two or more sorts of atoms bonded together.

8 Materials

8.1 Elements and compounds

Elements

(a) An element is a substance which cannot be broken down by chemical action into anything simpler. Many elements exist in nature as molecules, that is two or more atoms of the same element joined together.

Gold, silver and copper are the only metals found as elements in nature.

Compounds

(b) A compound is a combination of two or more elements. Compounds can only be broken down by chemical reactions. Compounds are always molecules; water molecules consist of two atoms of hydrogen joined to a single oxygen atom.

Is it an element or a compound?

(c)

element	compound
copper	sugar
iron	water
zinc	rust
sulphur	salt
uranium	hydrochloric acid
argon	carbon dioxide
arsenic	

(d) No. Compounds cannot be broken up by dissolving them. After the water had evaporated you would be left with the original compound.

Molecules

(e) A molecule of an element consists of one or more atoms of that element, e.g. a molecule of oxygen is made up of two atoms of oxygen. A molecule of ozone is made up of one molecule of ordinary oxygen plus a single atom of oxygen making a three-atom molecule of oxygen.

Refer to the ozone layer in 6.4 (f).

The molecule of a compound consists of one or more atoms of the elements which make up the compound. So a molecule of methane consists of one atom of carbon joined to four atoms of hydrogen.

Elements react to give compounds.

(f) *hydrogen and oxygen:* water.
carbon and oxygen: carbon dioxide or carbon monoxide.
sodium and chlorine: common salt (sodium chloride).
silicon and oxygen: silica or quartz.
sulphur and oxygen: sulphur dioxide.

8.2 Chemical reactions

(a) All hydrocarbon fuels are made up from carbon and hydrogen.

(b) Other hydrocarbon fuels include:

coal   paraffin   methane   oil   petrol   wood

(c) All hydrocarbons react with oxygen in the same way:
hydrogen + oxygen = water
carbon + oxygen = carbon dioxide

(d) $CH_4 + 2O_2 \rightarrow CO_2 + 2H_2O$. You could also view this as two separate reactions: $2H + O \rightarrow H_2O$ and $C + 2O \rightarrow CO_2$.

(e) Children will say that you cannot see candle wax burning. Soak a dead match in liquid wax then light it. The match cannot burn but the wax does.

Children will say that the liquid wax does not seem to burn. Blow out the candle flame and immediately relight the white 'smoke' to show that the wax vapour burns.

A candle wick is made of string. Look at how feebly a piece of string on its own burns.

Processes at work when a candle burns

(f) You would produce a mass of carbon dioxide and water which is greater than the mass of wax you started with. This is because you are adding oxygen to the hydrocarbon when it burns.

(g) It is true that most burning reactions cannot be reversed – wood ash and the other products of burning cannot be remade into wood. However, the burning of hydrogen in oxygen produces water, and you can reverse this reaction by passing an electrical current through water. This process is called electrolysis.

Side labels:
What is wax?

Fuels

Burning reactions

Candle wick myths

Reversible burning?

Respiration	(h) When you digest food it is broken up to allow it to pass from the gut into the bloodstream.

Digestion is slow oxidization or slow burning.

Plant reactions

It is then passed into the cells of the body where oxygen combines with the food to give energy. The main waste products are carbon dioxide and water.

(i) Photosynthesis.

(j) In the course of digestion $C_6H_{12}O_6$ is broken down and combined with oxygen to give carbon dioxide and water. These are the materials which plants need to make glucose in the first place.

Carbon is circulated by plants and animals.

Melting and evaporating

8.3 Physical changes: melting, freezing, evaporating and dissolving
(a) An input of heat energy is needed to make the change from solid to liquid to gas.

See 8.2 (g) on burning reactions.

Heat needs to be extracted to accomplish the changes from gas to liquid to solid.

(b) The temperature of the ice increases steadily until it reaches 0°C. At this point there is still solid ice and all the heat energy is used to turn the ice from a solid to a liquid – the energy is needed to break the bonds.

Once all the ice has turned to water the temperature increases until it reaches boiling point. The water stays at that point. The heat energy goes into breaking the bonds between the water molecules which then turn into molecules of water vapour.

Molecules of water

(c) No. Water molecules stay as water molecules no matter how cold or hot they get.

Why does ice float?

(d) The molecules in water when it is in the form of ice are spaced further apart than when it is in liquid form. This makes ice unlike all other solids.

If ice was denser than water it would sink and lakes would freeze from the bottom up.

The molecules of water (after it has reached 4°C) get further apart (water expands as it warms) until it reaches 100°C. When water changes to a vapour the molecules can spread out to fill any container.

Evaporation

(e) Water evaporates quickly when:

the surrounding air is dry. Air which is saturated with water (high humidity) will not absorb any more water.

See the connection with saturation (f) below.

the air is moving thus preventing any one part of it getting saturated.

the air is warm.

Words to do with dissolving

(f) *solution:* a solid dissolved in a liquid, e.g. copper sulphate will dissolve in water. The solid never settles out and cannot be filtered.

Solutions are transparent. All of the others are cloudy.

solvent: the liquid in which the solid is dissolved, e.g. fat will dissolve in dry-cleaning fluid.

suspension: a liquid with small particles of a solid suspended in it, e.g. a teaspoon of clay in a glass of water. Suspensions are cloudy. If left a suspension will settle out. The solid will be caught in a filter.

colloid: a solid which is dispersed in a liquid in the form of very small particles (but bigger than molecules), e.g. starch or glue in water. Colloids don't settle, can't be filtered and are always cloudy.

emulsion: an emulsion is formed when two liquids are mixed together, e.g. commercially produced French dressing.

saturated: there is a limit to the amount of a solid which can be dissolved in a liquid. When this limit is reached the solution is saturated, e.g. a salt solution is saturated with about 40 g in 100 ml of water; a sugar solution is saturated when 300 g have been dissolved in 100 ml of water.

> More sugar will dissolve in hot water than in cold. This isn't true of salt though.

Re-crystallization

(g) You need to evaporate the water, leaving the salt crystals behind. Water will change to a gas without being heated so long as the surrounding air is not saturated with water vapour.

Filtration

(h) No filter has been made which will allow a molecule of one specific type through but stop another. The salt particles in solution are simply too small to be caught in a filter.

Suspensions

(i) The mixture is cloudy and the flour begins to settle on the bottom. This is typical of all instances in which material is not dissolved. If you have ever made beer or wine at home you will know that sometimes it takes weeks for the yeast to settle to the bottom.

> Teacher demonstrations are essential.

(j) They confuse mixing-in with dissolving because superficially the flour looks as if it forms a solution – you can't see any lumps of dry power and for a while there is no flour on the bottom. Notice that in cold water and without stirring even salt can take a very long time to dissolve.

Coffee

(k) In the filter you trap the undissolved parts of the coffee bean. Dissolved material (which contains the colour, smell and taste) goes straight through the filter.

If a pot of coffee dries out the remains are the chemicals which were dissolved in the water.

> Don't bother to drink it as it tastes terrible.

If you then add water to the dried-out crust you will get a coffee solution again.

That, in essence, is how instant coffee is made.

....

8.4 The properties of solids, liquids and gases

Three states of matter

(a) Water is the only material which exists as solid, liquid and gas.

(b) *gas:* there is no force holding gas molecules together so they are free to move. A gas will fill any container into which it is placed.

liquid: a liquid has a definite volume but no fixed shape. The molecules of a liquid are held less strongly than those of a solid. You cannot cut a liquid and its surface is always level.

solid: a solid has a definite shape. It can be cut and it keeps its shape.

solid   liquid   gas

(c) You could weigh an empty balloon or ball then pump it up and reweigh it. The additional weight is that of the air you have added.

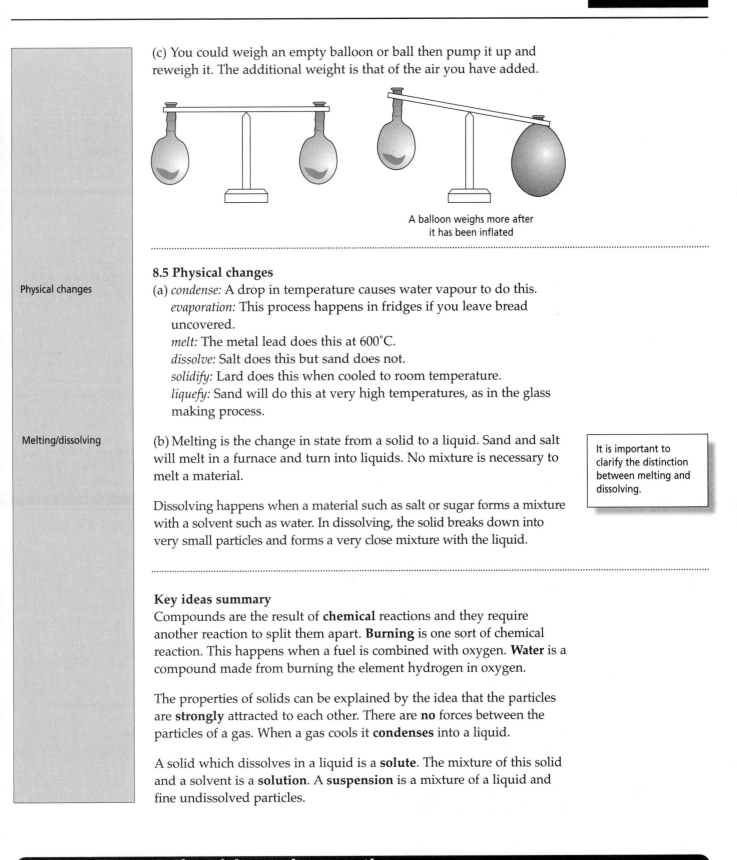

A balloon weighs more after
it has been inflated

8.5 Physical changes

Physical changes

(a) *condense:* A drop in temperature causes water vapour to do this.
evaporation: This process happens in fridges if you leave bread uncovered.
melt: The metal lead does this at 600°C.
dissolve: Salt does this but sand does not.
solidify: Lard does this when cooled to room temperature.
liquefy: Sand will do this at very high temperatures, as in the glass making process.

Melting/dissolving

(b) Melting is the change in state from a solid to a liquid. Sand and salt will melt in a furnace and turn into liquids. No mixture is necessary to melt a material.

> It is important to clarify the distinction between melting and dissolving.

Dissolving happens when a material such as salt or sugar forms a mixture with a solvent such as water. In dissolving, the solid breaks down into very small particles and forms a very close mixture with the liquid.

Key ideas summary

Compounds are the result of **chemical** reactions and they require another reaction to split them apart. **Burning** is one sort of chemical reaction. This happens when a fuel is combined with oxygen. **Water** is a compound made from burning the element hydrogen in oxygen.

The properties of solids can be explained by the idea that the particles are **strongly** attracted to each other. There are **no** forces between the particles of a gas. When a gas cools it **condenses** into a liquid.

A solid which dissolves in a liquid is a **solute**. The mixture of this solid and a solvent is a **solution**. A **suspension** is a mixture of a liquid and fine undissolved particles.

9 Electricity and magnetism

9.1 Conductors and insulators

Conductors

(a) Gold is the best conductor of electricity. Copper, aluminium, iron, mercury and steel (all metals) are good conductors.

Insulators

(b) Rubber, plastics, perspex, pottery.

Resistors	(c) Carbon, silicon, germanium, water and humans. The first three of these are called semi-conductors. Some solutions, such as salty water and acids, allow some electrical flow. Pure water is an insulator of electricity.
Explaining conduction	(d) Metals are good conductors because they contain many free electrons which are not attached to particular atoms. These electrons are free to move when electrical connections are made.

(d) Metals are good conductors because they contain many free electrons which are not attached to particular atoms. These electrons are free to move when electrical connections are made.

> Electrons are tiny, negatively charged particles.

The electrons in insulators are firmly bound into their atoms and are not free to move.

9.2 Current and flow

Flow of electricity

(a) Electrical flow is the movement of electrons through a conductor.

> An amazing number of electrons is involved.

An analogy for electrical flow

(b) To make water flow in the pipes there has to be a water pump. To make electricity flow through wires there has to be an electron pump. The battery acts like a pump forcing the electrons through the wires.

Electrons

(c) Electrons are pushed away from the negative end of a battery and attracted to the positive end. However, this fact wasn't known by the first electrical experimenters, who thought the direction of electron flow was positive to negative.

> The direction of electrical flow has little practical significance in the primary classroom.

The flow of electrons is the same throughout a series circuit.

Ammeters and electrical flow

(d) This is a series circuit. The flow of electrons throughout a series circuit is the same because it follows one route. There is no bunching of electrons anywhere in the circuit, and no deficit of electrons anywhere in the circuit. Using an ammeter to measure the flow of electricity in a series circuit will show that it is the same at any point.

> Think about the M25 with all the slip roads sealed off – that would act like a simple circuit.

However, in a parallel circuit the flow of electrons branches in places. Each branch of a parallel circuit takes a separate share of the current. (See section 9.4 (k).)

(e) The unit used to measure electrical flow is the amp (A).

(f) The following are all misconceptions:

> Use a similar technique to find out what older primary school children think.

The current flow is less in the return wire. This ignores the fact that electrons cannot leave the wire.

The return wire is not needed. What happens to the electrons when they get to the bulb?

The current moves along both wires and clashes in the middle causing the bulb to light. Electrons carry a negative charge. They are repelled by the negatively charged end of the battery and attracted by the positive end, causing flow in one direction only.

This is the only explanation which is correct:

The current is the same whether the wire is going to or returning from the bulb.

> Children's alternative constructs

A child's view of how current operates is often different from the scientist's. This example shows children's most frequent misconceptions.

9.3 Voltage

Potential difference

(a) Voltage is a measure of the energy of the flow of electricity.

(b) A voltmeter is wired in parallel to a device. This allows the voltmeter to compare the energy of the electricity at two different points in the circuit. This difference is called 'potential difference.'

An analogy for electricity flow

(c) Answers will vary. This is the analogy I use when describing the concept of voltage:

A garden has a series of artificial waterfalls. The waterfalls are in a circuit which also contains pools, and the flow of water through the circuit is driven by a pump.

The waterfalls are big users of energy in this circuit. They convert it into other forms of energy, like noise and movement. The bigger the waterfall, the more energy it is able to convert.

The amount of water flowing through this circuit is the current. The height the water reaches before it begins its descent is the voltage; this is the energy available to the circuit. When the water reaches the bottom pool and returns to the pump, it has no energy (0 volts) left.

The pump acts like a battery. It pushes the water on, recharging it to complete the circuit again. Sometimes the pump runs down. When this happens the amount of energy it can give to the water will be less than the circuit needs to function properly. The waterfalls run at a trickle. Sometimes they stop altogether.

> This is an analogy of the way that voltage and flow work.

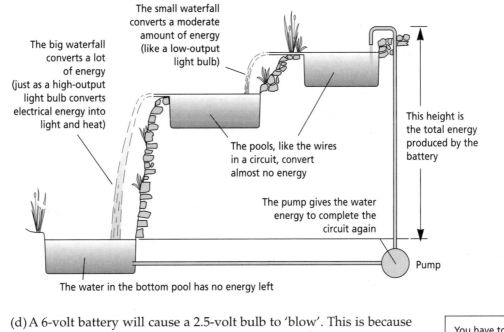

The small waterfall converts a moderate amount of energy (like a low-output light bulb)

The big waterfall converts a lot of energy (just as a high-output light bulb converts electrical energy into light and heat)

The pools, like the wires in a circuit, convert almost no energy

This height is the total energy produced by the battery

The pump gives the water energy to complete the circuit again

Pump

The water in the bottom pool has no energy left

Match the voltage of bulb and battery.

(d) A 6-volt battery will cause a 2.5-volt bulb to 'blow'. This is because the electrical flow has too much energy for the filament, causing it to overheat and melt. The battery voltage must be the same as or less than the bulb voltage.

> You have to match the voltage of the battery to the voltage printed on the bulb.

Electrical energy

(e) Joule (J).

....

9.4 Resistance

Electrical flow through conductors

(a) ← Electrons moving this way   ← Electrons moving this way

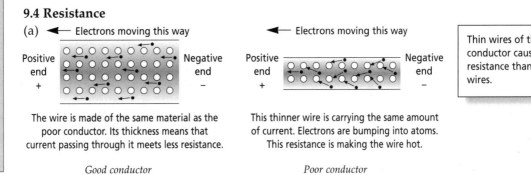

Positive end +   Negative end −   Positive end +   Negative end −

The wire is made of the same material as the poor conductor. Its thickness means that current passing through it meets less resistance.

This thinner wire is carrying the same amount of current. Electrons are bumping into atoms. This resistance is making the wire hot.

Good conductor   *Poor conductor*

> Thin wires of the same conductor cause more resistance than thick wires.

The parts of a bulb

(b)

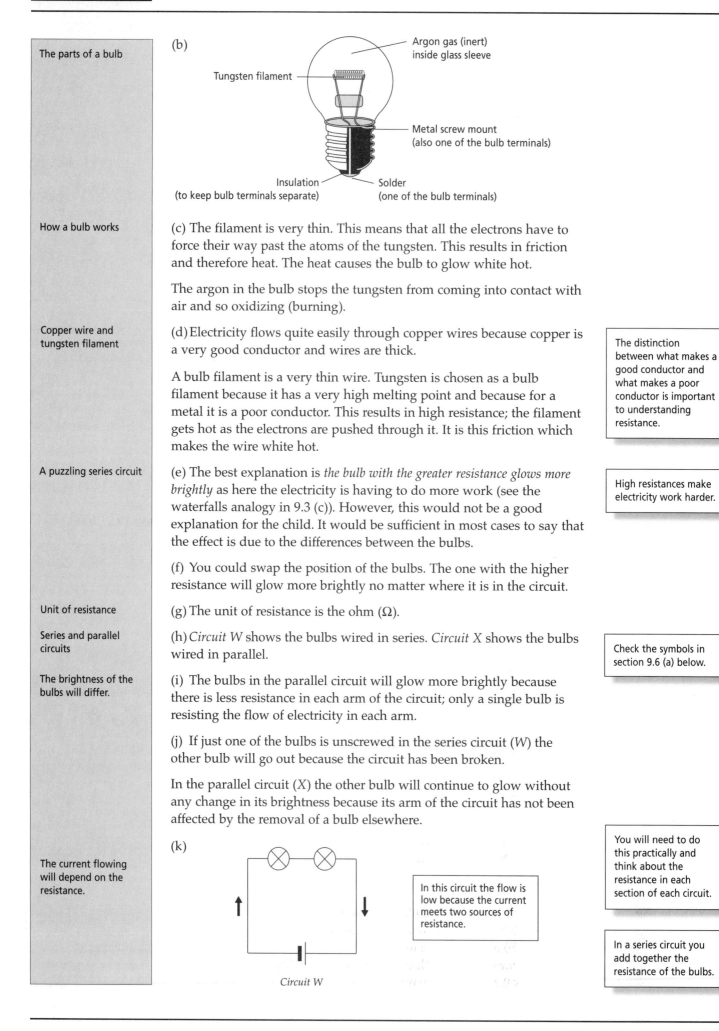

Argon gas (inert) inside glass sleeve

Tungsten filament

Metal screw mount (also one of the bulb terminals)

Insulation (to keep bulb terminals separate)

Solder (one of the bulb terminals)

How a bulb works

(c) The filament is very thin. This means that all the electrons have to force their way past the atoms of the tungsten. This results in friction and therefore heat. The heat causes the bulb to glow white hot.

The argon in the bulb stops the tungsten from coming into contact with air and so oxidizing (burning).

Copper wire and tungsten filament

(d) Electricity flows quite easily through copper wires because copper is a very good conductor and wires are thick.

A bulb filament is a very thin wire. Tungsten is chosen as a bulb filament because it has a very high melting point and because for a metal it is a poor conductor. This results in high resistance; the filament gets hot as the electrons are pushed through it. It is this friction which makes the wire white hot.

> The distinction between what makes a good conductor and what makes a poor conductor is important to understanding resistance.

A puzzling series circuit

(e) The best explanation is *the bulb with the greater resistance glows more brightly* as here the electricity is having to do more work (see the waterfalls analogy in 9.3 (c)). However, this would not be a good explanation for the child. It would be sufficient in most cases to say that the effect is due to the differences between the bulbs.

> High resistances make electricity work harder.

(f) You could swap the position of the bulbs. The one with the higher resistance will glow more brightly no matter where it is in the circuit.

Unit of resistance

(g) The unit of resistance is the ohm (Ω).

Series and parallel circuits

(h) *Circuit W* shows the bulbs wired in series. *Circuit X* shows the bulbs wired in parallel.

> Check the symbols in section 9.6 (a) below.

The brightness of the bulbs will differ.

(i) The bulbs in the parallel circuit will glow more brightly because there is less resistance in each arm of the circuit; only a single bulb is resisting the flow of electricity in each arm.

(j) If just one of the bulbs is unscrewed in the series circuit (*W*) the other bulb will go out because the circuit has been broken.

In the parallel circuit (*X*) the other bulb will continue to glow without any change in its brightness because its arm of the circuit has not been affected by the removal of a bulb elsewhere.

(k)

The current flowing will depend on the resistance.

> You will need to do this practically and think about the resistance in each section of each circuit.

In this circuit the flow is low because the current meets two sources of resistance.

> In a series circuit you add together the resistance of the bulbs.

Circuit W

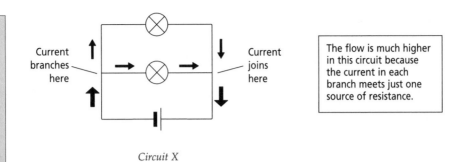

The flow is much higher in this circuit because the current in each branch meets just one source of resistance.

Circuit X

More current is flowing through each bulb in the parallel circuit (X). Remember that the bulbs are glowing more brightly in this circuit and this shows that more current is flowing through each bulb.

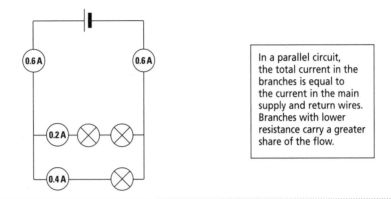

In a parallel circuit, the total current in the branches is equal to the current in the main supply and return wires. Branches with lower resistance carry a greater share of the flow.

9.5 Power

Electrical energy

(a) Electricity can be changed into heat, movement, magnetism, light and sound.

Different rates of energy use

(b) 1 electric kettle 2 light bulb 3 torch 4 pocket calculator.

Power

(c) *Power* is the rate at which energy is changed. Watt (W) is the SI unit of power. A 100 W light bulb changes electricity four times as quickly as a 25 W bulb. Look at the information on items like vacuum cleaners and kettles for their rating in watts.

See section 2.9 for SI units.

River analogy

(d) You work out the power of an energy source by calculating the amount of work that it can do. In electrical terms you need to know:

the amount of current flow (measured in amps)
the pressure of the current (measured in volts).

To work out power you multiply current (amps) by voltage
watts = amps × volts

In a river the flow is like current, the fall of the river is like voltage, the ability to drive a waterwheel is like power.

Torch bulb power

(e) 0.3 A × 3 V = 0.9 watts
   0.2 A × 6 V = 1.2 watts (uses most power)
   0.1 A × 3 V = 0.3 watts (uses least power)

Kilowatt

(f) 1000

Calculating watts

(g) 100 W × 1 hour = one tenth of a unit = 0.6p
   60 W × 5 hours = three tenths of a unit = 1.8p
   10 W × 50 hours = half a unit = 3p
   3 kW × for 0.1 hours = three tenths of a unit = 1.8p
   10 kW × 0.2 hours = two units = 12p

Use this information to help plan economical electricity use.

(h) hours in use = 365 × 5 = 1825 hours

1825 × 0.1 (the units per hour used by a 100 W bulb)

= 182.5 units × 6p per unit = £10.95 per year.

The energy saving bulb uses one-fifth of the power, £2.19 of electricity per year, so it will save £8.76 per year minus the cost of the original bulb. (Remember that each energy saving bulb lasts five times as long as the standard bulb.)

9.6 Circuit symbols and diagrams

(a)

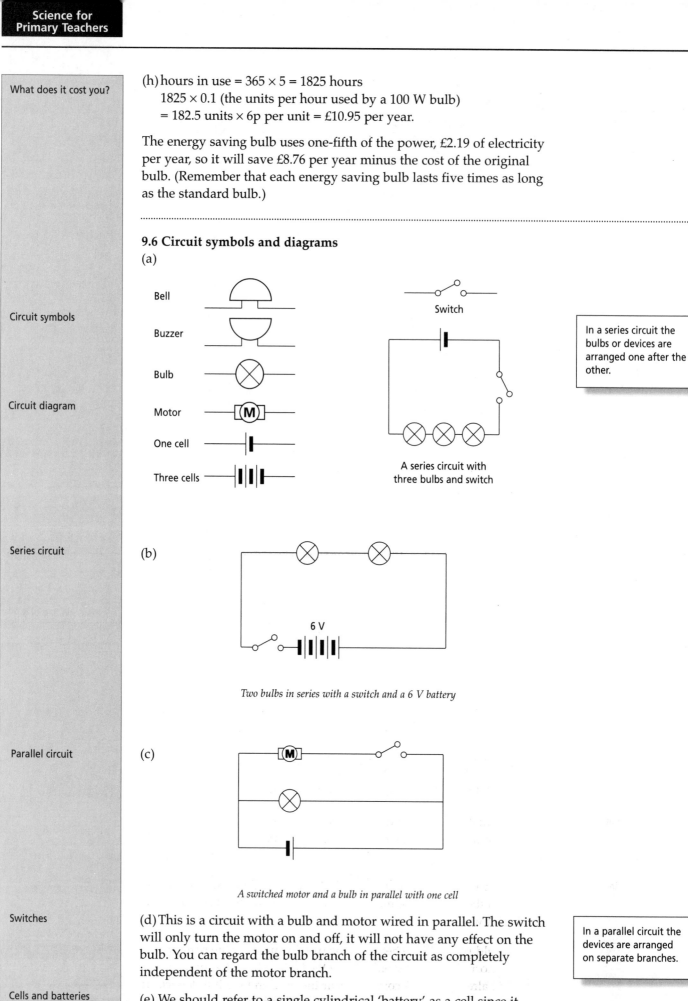

A series circuit with three bulbs and switch

> In a series circuit the bulbs or devices are arranged one after the other.

(b)

Two bulbs in series with a switch and a 6 V battery

(c)

A switched motor and a bulb in parallel with one cell

(d) This is a circuit with a bulb and motor wired in parallel. The switch will only turn the motor on and off, it will not have any effect on the bulb. You can regard the bulb branch of the circuit as completely independent of the motor branch.

> In a parallel circuit the devices are arranged on separate branches.

(e) We should refer to a single cylindrical 'battery' as a cell since it contains two metals in a container which is filled with an acid or alkali.

(f) You could make a cell by putting pieces of zinc and copper in a glass of vinegar. The metals must not touch.

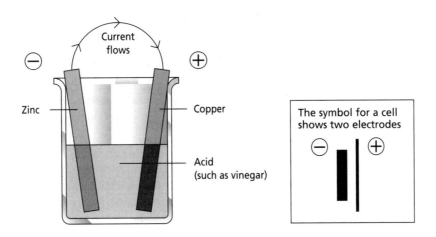

The symbol for a cell shows two electrodes

A simple primary cell

(g) A battery is a group of cells connected together (i.e. in a combination or 'battery').

9.7 Magnetism

(a) Like poles repel and unlike poles attract.

(b) The north pole of this magnet will point north because it is attracted by the magnetic field of the Earth.

(c) If like poles repel, logically the magnetic north pole of the Earth should be a magnetic south pole to attract the north pole of your bar magnet.

In fact, the problem is one of naming. Sailors have given the name 'north' to the end of the compass needle which **points** north. This is why the north pole of a magnet is called north.

> This is a good example of how everyday use of words gets tangled up with scientific use.

(d) Magnets will attract objects on a school desk. The Earth's magnetic field works all over the Earth.

(e) High voltages, such as those in cables used to carry electricity over long distances, produce strong magnetic fields. Some people believe that these fields have adverse effects on the health of people.

(f) Coil insulated wire round a large metal nail and pass a current through the wire. You can increase the effect by using a more powerful battery or by winding more loops of wire round the nail.

> More electrical power means greater effect.

(g) The bulb is a resistor, so the electrical current will be cut down by its presence in the circuit. The more current available to the electromagnet, the better it will work.

> The bulb is in series with the electromagnet. It has much more resistance than the electromagnet.

(h) You could place a wire between the two terminals of the battery (this is a circuit and would cause the battery to go flat quickly if it wasn't flat already). Put a compass near the wire and see if it deflects at all. If it doesn't move, put the compass in a box and wind wire round it. This will amplify any magnetic effect if there is one to detect.

Key ideas summary
Electrons are involved in carrying electrical charge through a
conductor. If they encounter difficulty in flowing the material is a poor
conductor of charge. Poor conductors are referred to as **resistors**. When
a current passes through a poor conductor the material heats up and
may glow white hot. This happens usefully in a bulb **filament**. A
battery pushes electrons round a circuit – the force of the push is
measured in **volts** and the amount of flow is measured in **amps**. The
power of a current is found by multiplying the flow (**amps**) by the force
(**volts**) to give power in watts. Low energy light bulbs operate at the
same **voltage** as ordinary light bulbs (240 volts) but they allow only
relatively small flows of electricity through them.

Magnetic effect can be produced by a **current** flowing in a wire.
Magnets have two poles. Like poles of a magnet **repel**.

10 Energy

10.1 Energy, force and fuel

Examples of force, fuel
and energy

(a) The unit in which each is measured is shown in brackets.

> *a man pushing a car:*
> force = push from man (newtons)
> fuel = food eaten by man (joules)
> energy = equivalent to the distance moved by the car (joules).

> *the wind turning a windmill:*
> force = push of wind (newtons)
> fuel = heat from the sun (causing wind) (joules)
> energy = the work which the grindstones can do (joules).

> *a rocket taking off:*
> force = push from motors (newtons)
> fuel = chemical fuel on board (joules)
> energy = equivalent to the distance moved by the rocket (joules).

Newton is the measure
of force (see section
11.1, Measuring force).

Joule was from
Bradford in spite of his
French-sounding name
(see section 11.1).

Joules are the measure
of energy and fuel.
Fuels are a form of
chemical energy.

Body fuel

(b) Food. We break down food in our stomach and digestive system
(this stage requires an input of energy). When the food is combined
with oxygen in our cells energy is released.

10.2 Generating electricity

Power station

(a) The fossil fuel – coal, oil, gas or peat – is burnt to release heat. The
heat boils water to produce steam. The steam rushes past propellers
called turbines, causing the propellers to turn. The turbines turn the
generators which produce electricity.

The energy changes in
a car engine are similar
except that hot gas
takes the place of
steam.

Types of energy

(b) *Chemical energy* in the fuel is changed into *heat energy* when burnt.
The *heat energy* is turned into the *kinetic energy* of the steam and
turbines and this produces *electrical energy*.

Nuclear power

(c) As uranium decays it loses particles. In the process it produces a great
deal of heat which is used to make steam to drive generator turbines.

This is nuclear fission.

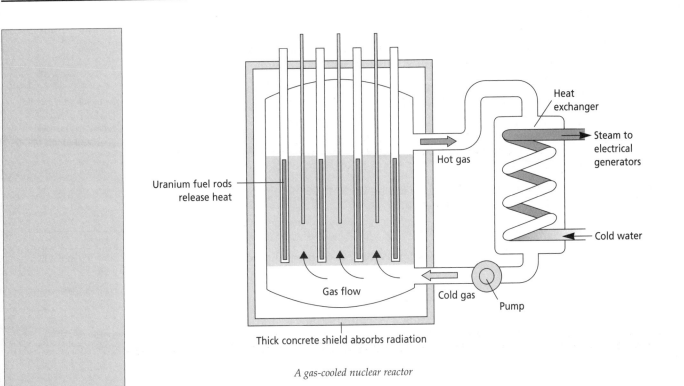

A gas-cooled nuclear reactor

10.3 Biological and chemical energy

(a) Carbon combines with oxygen. Energy is required to form the bond, but this is less than the energy contained in the bonds of the hydrocarbon, so there is a net release of energy from the reaction.

(b) Plants trap the energy of the sun in the chemical bonds of glucose. The trapped energy is released when the plant respires (combines the carbon and hydrogen with oxygen).

(c) Food is burnt in a device called a calorimeter. Heat released by the burning food is used to heat water and calculations are made based on how hot the water becomes. A leaf of lettuce will hardly produce any heat but oil will burn to heat a teaspoon of water to near boiling point.

(d) You can try this in the classroom by burning a peanut under a tube or spoon of water. It is possible to boil a small quantity of water. **Take care with children who are allergic to peanuts.**

> Some energy has to go into separating the carbon from its hydrocarbon compound, in the same way that food needs energy input to break it down.

> Fats and oils are burnt as fuels as well as eaten for food.

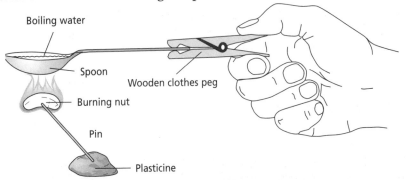

10.4 Energy resources

(a) *kinetic energy:* movement energy, e.g. a person running has kinetic energy.

   chemical energy: the energy locked up in chemical compounds, e.g. food and fuel have chemical energy.

> You get hot when running; that's where most of the energy goes.

gravitational potential energy: the energy of an object which is high up, e.g. a bike at the top of a hill has gravitational potential energy which will turn to kinetic energy as it rolls downhill.

strain potential energy: the energy of a stretched spring or elastic, e.g. a bouncy ball dropped on the floor has strain potential energy; it changes shape when it hits the floor then springs back into its original shape which gives it the energy to leave the ground.

heat energy: the energy possessed by hot things, e.g. the sun.

A spit of fat is hot but has little energy. A radiator is relatively cool but has lots of energy.

Energy changes

(b) The chemical energy in the food eaten by the person who is firing the stone into the air:

changes to the kinetic energy of the person's moving arm

changes to the strain potential energy of the pulled elastic of the catapult

Write out some more energy changes like these.

changes to the kinetic energy of the stone leaving the catapult

changes to the gravitational potential energy of the stone high up

changes to the kinetic energy of the falling stone.

Heat is generated at every stage in this process.

Which fuels are renewable?

(c) *wood:* renewable.
   coal: fossil.
   oil: fossil.
   sugar cane: renewable.
   wind: renewable.
   peat: renewable (as claimed by the peat producers, who point to Russia as an example of a region where new peat is being created in peat bogs. New peat is not being created in most British bogs).

Burnt fuel

(d) All fuels are changed into heat. It is very difficult to concentrate heat since heat always moves from a hot place to a cooler place.

Key ideas summary

Energy can be **changed (turned)** from one form into another. You power your body with **chemical** energy (food) which is turned into movement, noise and heat. All the food energy is eventually dissipated as **heat**. It is difficult to reconcentrate the **heat** again. Energy in the form of **fuels** can be burnt to produce heat to make steam (moving energy) which makes **electricity** in generators.

Another sequence of energy changes can be found in a catapult: food – **movement** – elastic strain energy – **movement** – heat (friction) and **sound** (which changes into heat from the friction between the air molecules).

11 Forces

Unit of force

11.1 Measuring force
(a) Force is measured in newtons (N).

Simple calculations

(b) One newton (1 N)
    Three newtons (3 N)

Work

(c) A mass of 500 g = 5 newtons
5 N × 2 metres = 10 joules

The bag needs a force of 4 N
4 N × 3 metres = 12 joules

Remember that one newton is the force of gravity pulling on one 100 g apple (a Newton's Wonder, no doubt!)

How can you recognize balanced forces?

11.2 Balanced forces

(a) There are many possible instances. When you travel on a smoothly running train, car or plane you will notice that at a constant speed you do not get pushed back, thrown forward or from side to side.

Do this experiment in your imagination: Sit on a plane flying at 700 km/h or a train travelling smoothly at 175 km/h. Put on eye shades and headphones. Fall asleep. When you wake up would you know if you were stationary or whether you were moving quickly?

Experiments such as this are useful when studying forces.

Moving at a steady 700 km/h, you will feel no sensation of moving at speed. All forces on you, the passenger, are balanced.

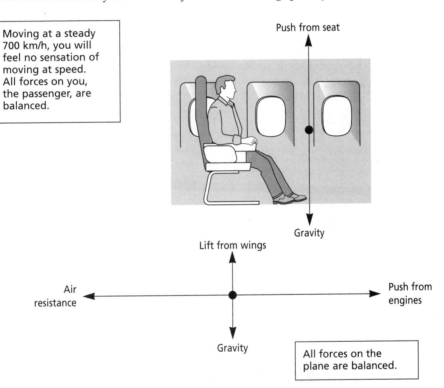

All forces on the plane are balanced.

Are these balanced?

(b) Balanced
a boat floating (upthrust from the water balances the weight).
a hot air balloon hovering (upthrust from the air balances the weight).
a ball on the ground (push from the ground balances the weight).
a feather falling at a constant speed (the air resistance balances the pull of gravity).
a jet cruising at a constant 500 km/h (air resistance is balanced by the push from the engines).
a ball rolling down a slope at a constant speed (the pull of gravity and friction are balanced).

Unbalanced
a hot air balloon rising (upthrust from the air is greater than the weight).
a ball after it has been struck by a tennis racquet (air resistance and gravity are slowing the ball; no other forces are acting).
a drag-racing car accelerating (the push from the engine is greater than friction and air resistance).

The push up from water is called upthrust.

Very light objects displace large volumes of air and get upthrust from the air.

Unbalanced forces cause things to speed up or slow down.

Floating

(c) An object floats when the upthrust from the water is equal to the object's weight. Upthrust depends on the volume of water displaced by the object.

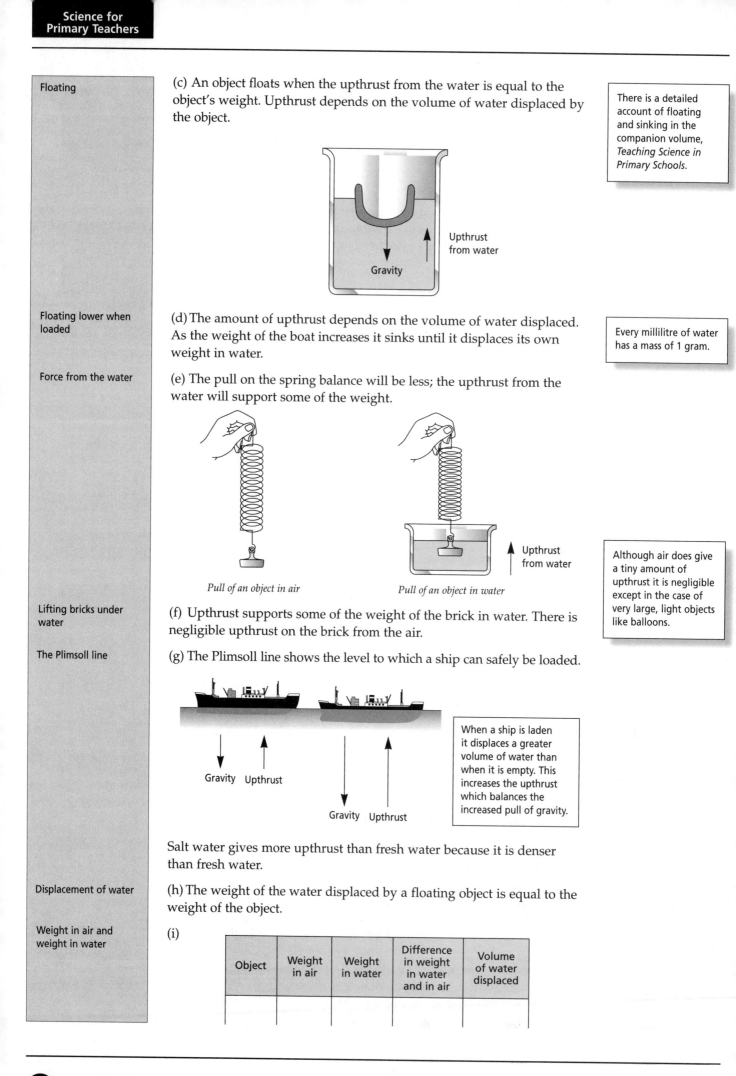

Upthrust from water

Gravity

There is a detailed account of floating and sinking in the companion volume, *Teaching Science in Primary Schools*.

Floating lower when loaded

(d) The amount of upthrust depends on the volume of water displaced. As the weight of the boat increases it sinks until it displaces its own weight in water.

Every millilitre of water has a mass of 1 gram.

Force from the water

(e) The pull on the spring balance will be less; the upthrust from the water will support some of the weight.

Pull of an object in air   *Pull of an object in water*

Upthrust from water

Although air does give a tiny amount of upthrust it is negligible except in the case of very large, light objects like balloons.

Lifting bricks under water

(f) Upthrust supports some of the weight of the brick in water. There is negligible upthrust on the brick from the air.

The Plimsoll line

(g) The Plimsoll line shows the level to which a ship can safely be loaded.

Gravity   Upthrust

Gravity   Upthrust

When a ship is laden it displaces a greater volume of water than when it is empty. This increases the upthrust which balances the increased pull of gravity.

Salt water gives more upthrust than fresh water because it is denser than fresh water.

Displacement of water

(h) The weight of the water displaced by a floating object is equal to the weight of the object.

Weight in air and weight in water

(i)

Object	Weight in air	Weight in water	Difference in weight in water and in air	Volume of water displaced

You will need to measure the volume in ml and the weight in newtons (N). However, the children will be much more familiar with measuring in grams and the results in grams can easily be converted to newtons. Do you want to be scientifically correct or more easily understood?

How do submarines dive and rise?

(j) The upthrust on a submarine floating on the surface is equal to its weight.

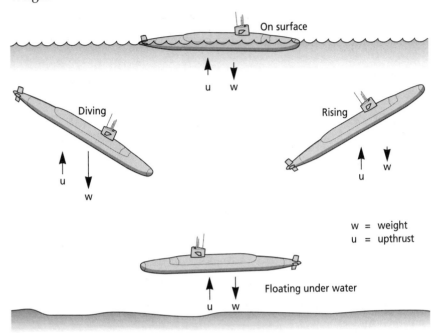

Submarines float under water. So do fish. Things are considered to have sunk only when they are touching the bottom.

When a submarine dives it floods its tanks to make itself heavier than the water (denser than the water).

To float underwater the submarine adjusts its tanks to make itself the same weight (same density) as water. The forces of upthrust and weight are equal.

To rise, the submarine empties its tanks. This makes the upthrust on the submarine greater than its weight, so the submarine moves upwards.

....

11.3 Unbalanced forces

(a) When a train, car or plane accelerates you feel yourself being pushed back. When it slows down you feel yourself being thrown forward. Turning pushes you to one side or another.

Seat belts stop you moving forward after the car has stopped.

(b)

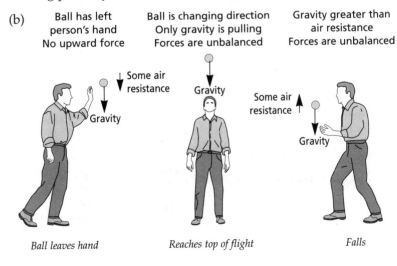

Ball leaves hand   Reaches top of flight   Falls

Remember that there is no force upward on a ball once it has left your hand.

There are unbalanced forces in **each** diagram. Remember that in its flight the ball is slowing (on its way up), changing direction (at the top of its flight) or accelerating (on its way down).

In each diagram the force of gravity is pulling the ball down. This force and air resistance slow the ball in the first diagram. There is no force in the direction of movement as the ball moves upwards. In fact, it is slowing all the time so there are unbalanced forces slowing it.

Spot the unbalanced forces.

> Many people think that forces operate in the direction of motion. This is not always the case.

In the second diagram only gravity is pulling; it is making the ball change direction.

In the final diagram gravity pulls down and air resistance operates against it.

Unbalanced forces?

(c) *a golf ball sitting on the tee:* balanced (there is no movement).

> No movement, or movement at constant speed in a straight line, is balanced force.

a golf ball in the process of being hit: unbalanced (the ball is speeding up from a standstill as the club pushes it).

a golf ball just after being hit: unbalanced (the ball is slowing down as air resistance and gravity pull on it; remember, it has left the club so nothing is pushing it in the direction of movement).

a golf ball rolling to a standstill on the green: unbalanced (the ball is slowing under the influence of the force of friction).

> Acceleration or slowing down or change of direction is unbalanced force.

a ballet dancer on points: balanced (no movement).

a dancer leaping: unbalanced (the dancer is changing speed and direction).

a trolley being pushed at a constant speed: balanced (the push from the shopper is equal to the force of friction).

a trolley rolling to a standstill: unbalanced (the push from the shopper is now less than the force of friction).

(d)

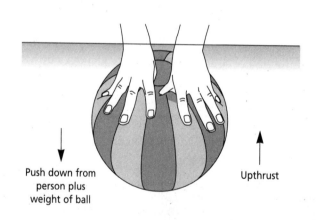

Push down from person plus weight of ball   Upthrust

Upward forces in a swimming pool

The force of upthrust makes it difficult to hold a large beach ball under water. When you let it go the upward push of the ball displacing its own volume of water is much greater than the pull of gravity, so the ball rushes upwards.

> It is also very hard to make yourself sink to the bottom of a swimming pool and stay there.

Forces on a party balloon

(e) The balloon will float upwards and away. This is because the balloon is lighter than the surrounding air. This results in the push from the air (upthrust, just the same as for water) being greater than the pull of gravity.

Balancing the forces on the balloon

(f) You would need to weight the balloon. This would result in the pull of gravity being larger than the upthrust from the air.

(g) To make the balloon hover at eye level you could add pieces of Blu Tack to it until it floated steadily. In terms of forces this would mean that the pull of gravity was equal to the upthrust from the air.

Attach a long piece of cotton to the balloon – just in case it rises to the ceiling and gets out of reach!

11.4 Friction

Measuring friction

(a) You could drag the box using a spring balance calibrated in newtons (a forcemeter). You would need to ensure that the box was moving at a constant speed.

Brakes

(b) The friction between the brake blocks and the wheel rim is used to slow a bicycle.

Friction enables walking.

(c) It would be impossible for you to walk without friction between your foot and the ground. As you push back with your foot when walking, friction pushes in the opposite direction. This is why it is so difficult to walk on ice – there is insufficient force pushing back against your foot.

(d)

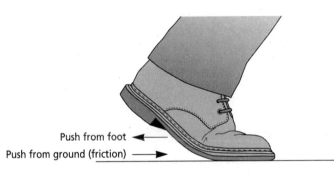

Push from foot ←
Push from ground (friction) →

11.5 Air resistance

Dropping sheets of paper

(a) The screwed up ball falls faster. Both pieces of paper have the same mass so the pull of gravity is equal on both. The screwed up ball has less air resistance and therefore falls faster.

(b)

Free-falling parachutes

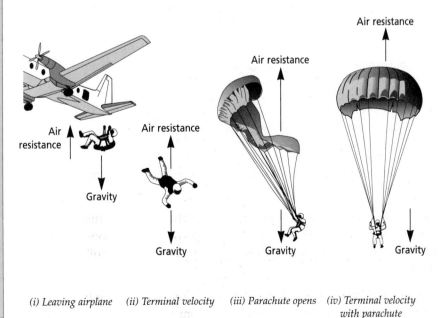

(i) Leaving airplane   *(ii) Terminal velocity*   *(iii) Parachute opens*   *(iv) Terminal velocity with parachute*

(c) In diagrams (*i*) and (*iii*) the forces are unbalanced because the parachutist is either accelerating or slowing down.

(d) In (*ii*) and (*iv*) the forces are balanced because the parachutist is falling at a constant speed.

(e) People find the idea of balanced forces in (*ii*) and (*iv*) difficult to accept because the parachutist continues to fall even though the force of air resistance is equal to the pull of gravity. We need to remember that the parachutist was **already falling** when the forces became equal.

11.6 Mass, gravity and weight

(a) *mass:* the amount of material (atoms) that there is in an object. This amount does not change unless some material is removed.

weight: the pull of gravity on a mass. The weight of an object changes as the pull of gravity changes. Objects weigh less on the moon because there is less gravity on the moon than on Earth.

gravity: the force of attraction between any two objects which have mass. All large masses (like planets and mountains) have a substantial gravitational pull.

> The everyday use of 'mass' and 'weight' is quite different from the way scientists use the same words.

(b) Nothing; it would remain the same.

(c) On the moon you would weigh one sixth of your weight on Earth. The pull of gravity on the surface of the moon is one sixth of the pull of gravity on Earth.

You know that astronauts are not weightless on the moon because they cannot leap off into space; the gravity of the moon always pulls them back again.

> The gravity of the moon causes the tides on Earth, giving proof that there is gravity on the moon.

(d) Your weight would be greater because of the extra gravitational pull of the planet.

(e) Gravity pulls harder on the book – you can feel that – yet both objects would hit the ground at the same time.

This seems contradictory. However, a big mass requires a big force to make it move. The pull of gravity on objects is directly proportional to their mass. So an object with a mass of 4 kg will be pulled with a force of 40 N, whilst an object with a mass of 2 kg will be pulled with a force of 20 N.

(f) The two balls would fall at the same rate and hit the ground at the same time.

11.7 Speed, acceleration, distance and time

(a) 50 km per hour.

(b) The car was accelerating rapidly where the line on the graph is steep. It was accelerating slowly where the line is less steep.

(c) The average speed of the bus is the distance it travels divided by the time it takes to complete its journey. The speed at any one point in the journey is the distance travelled (say one metre) divided by the time it takes to travel that distance.

Acceleration is increase in velocity (speed in a particular direction) per second. If the bus increases its velocity from 20 metres per second to 30 metres per second over 5 seconds then its acceleration is equal to the increase in its velocity divided by the time this takes to achieve. In this case it is:

10 metres per second (the increase in velocity)
divided by 5 seconds (the time taken to increase the velocity)
= 2 metres increase in velocity per second in every second.

Key ideas summary

A **force** is a push or a pull. If all the forces acting on an object are **balanced** then the object stays still or moves at a constant speed in a constant direction. A stationary train has **balanced** forces acting on it. The same train travelling at a **constant** speed in a straight line also has balanced forces acting on it. Passengers do not feel pulls and pushes when the train is travelling at a constant speed nor when it is **still**. Objects which are floating in air or in **water** have **balanced** forces acting on them.

Unbalanced forces operate when the pulls or pushes are bigger in one direction than in another. This results in the object speeding up or **slowing** down. As a train accelerates or slows down passengers can feel the change in the forces on them.

Gravity pulls on masses. Mass is measured in grams and **kilograms**. The pull of gravity on these masses is called **weight** and is measured in **newtons**. Objects such as iron balls, which are fairly heavy for their surface area, will fall at the **same** speed if dropped from a fairly tall building. Air **resistance** is a force which **slows** moving objects. This has more effect on light objects as they fall through the **air** than it does on heavy objects.

When an object is placed in water it **displaces** some of the water. This is true both for objects which **sink** and those which float. When an object displaces water it is pushed up or supported by the **water**. This is true for floaters and sinkers. This 'push up' is called **buoyancy** or upthrust. The amount of upthrust is the same as the **weight of water** which is displaced by the object. This is true for floaters and sinkers.

An object which floats in water experiences an upthrust which is **equal** to its total weight. A floater is effectively weightless. The forces of **gravity** and upthrust are in balance. An object which sinks in water loses some **weight**. The weight lost by a sinker is equal to the weight of the water which the sinker **displaces**.

12 Light

12.1 Light travels

(a) You cannot see round corners.
   A torch beam is straight not curved.
   One object will block the visibility of another if both are in line.
   Shadows are in line with the object and the light source.
   Eclipses occur when the sun, Earth and moon are in line.

(b) Shadows are formed when an object blocks light. The area of blocked light is similar in shape to the blocking object.

(c) *Umbra* is the sharp dark shadow where the light from the source is completely blocked.

Straight lines and light

Shadows

Umbra and penumbra

Look in section 14.3 for the distinction between a solar and a lunar eclipse.

Rembrandt's paintings show that shadows are rarely black.

95

Penumbra is the semi-shadow area between the umbra and the edge of the shadow.

12.2 Colour and the properties of light

(a)

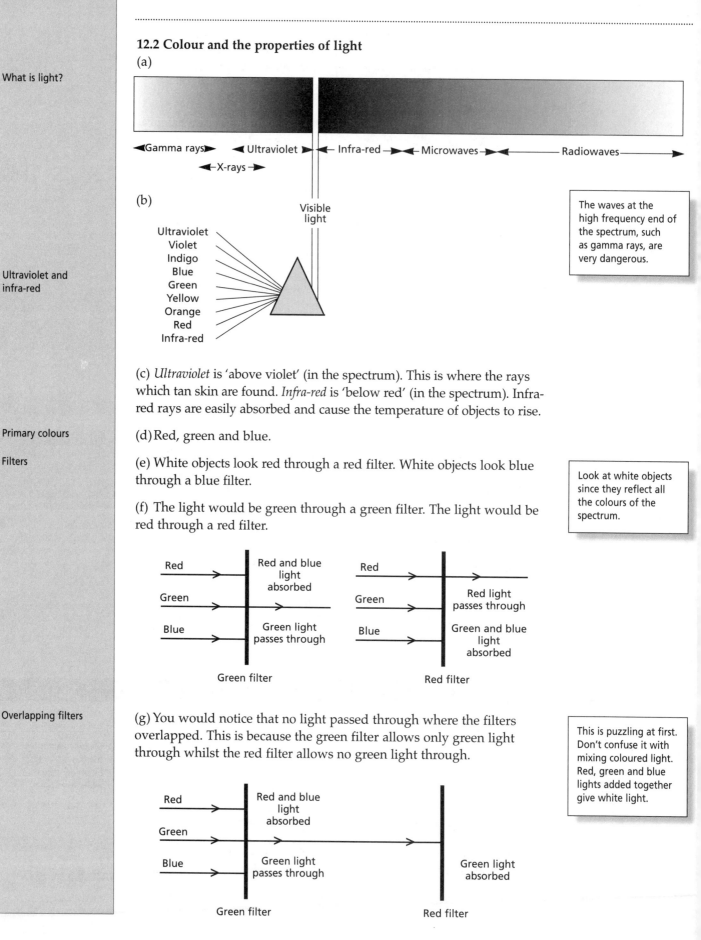

What is light?

Ultraviolet and infra-red

The waves at the high frequency end of the spectrum, such as gamma rays, are very dangerous.

(c) *Ultraviolet* is 'above violet' (in the spectrum). This is where the rays which tan skin are found. *Infra-red* is 'below red' (in the spectrum). Infrared rays are easily absorbed and cause the temperature of objects to rise.

Primary colours

(d) Red, green and blue.

Filters

(e) White objects look red through a red filter. White objects look blue through a blue filter.

Look at white objects since they reflect all the colours of the spectrum.

(f) The light would be green through a green filter. The light would be red through a red filter.

Overlapping filters

(g) You would notice that no light passed through where the filters overlapped. This is because the green filter allows only green light through whilst the red filter allows no green light through.

This is puzzling at first. Don't confuse it with mixing coloured light. Red, green and blue lights added together give white light.

(h) None of the light would pass through both filters together.

Coloured objects

(i) A blue car reflects blue light. It absorbs both the other primary colours.

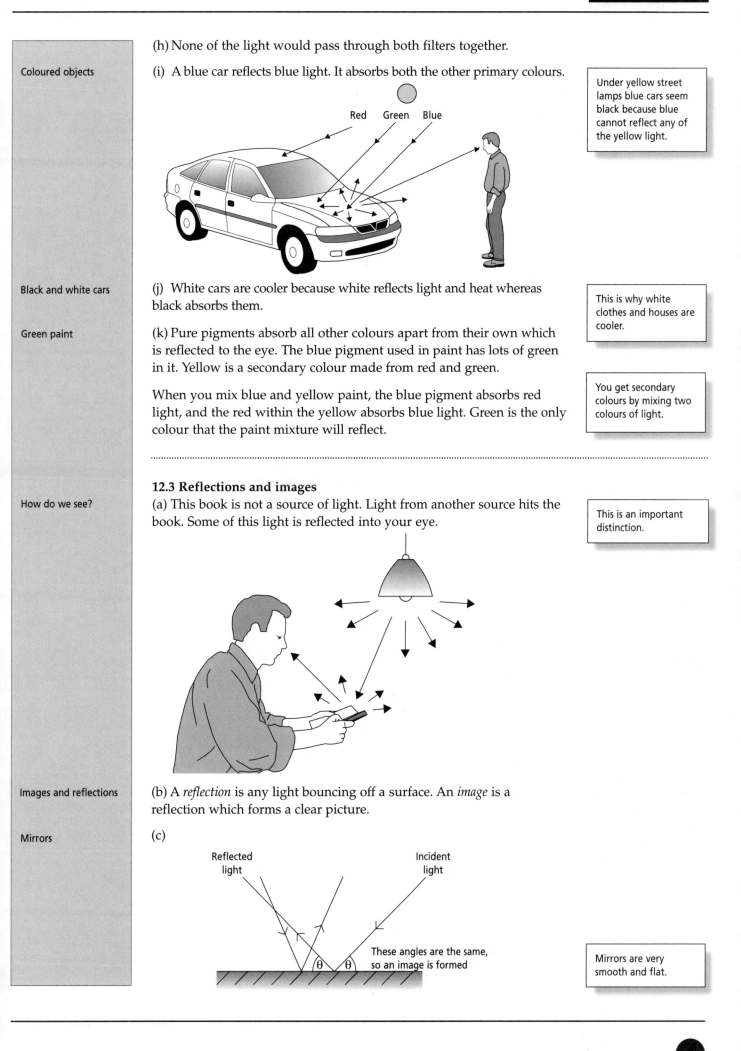

Red   Green   Blue

> Under yellow street lamps blue cars seem black because blue cannot reflect any of the yellow light.

Black and white cars

(j) White cars are cooler because white reflects light and heat whereas black absorbs them.

> This is why white clothes and houses are cooler.

Green paint

(k) Pure pigments absorb all other colours apart from their own which is reflected to the eye. The blue pigment used in paint has lots of green in it. Yellow is a secondary colour made from red and green.

When you mix blue and yellow paint, the blue pigment absorbs red light, and the red within the yellow absorbs blue light. Green is the only colour that the paint mixture will reflect.

> You get secondary colours by mixing two colours of light.

12.3 Reflections and images

How do we see?

(a) This book is not a source of light. Light from another source hits the book. Some of this light is reflected into your eye.

> This is an important distinction.

Images and reflections

(b) A *reflection* is any light bouncing off a surface. An *image* is a reflection which forms a clear picture.

Mirrors

(c)

Reflected light   Incident light

θ   θ   These angles are the same, so an image is formed

> Mirrors are very smooth and flat.

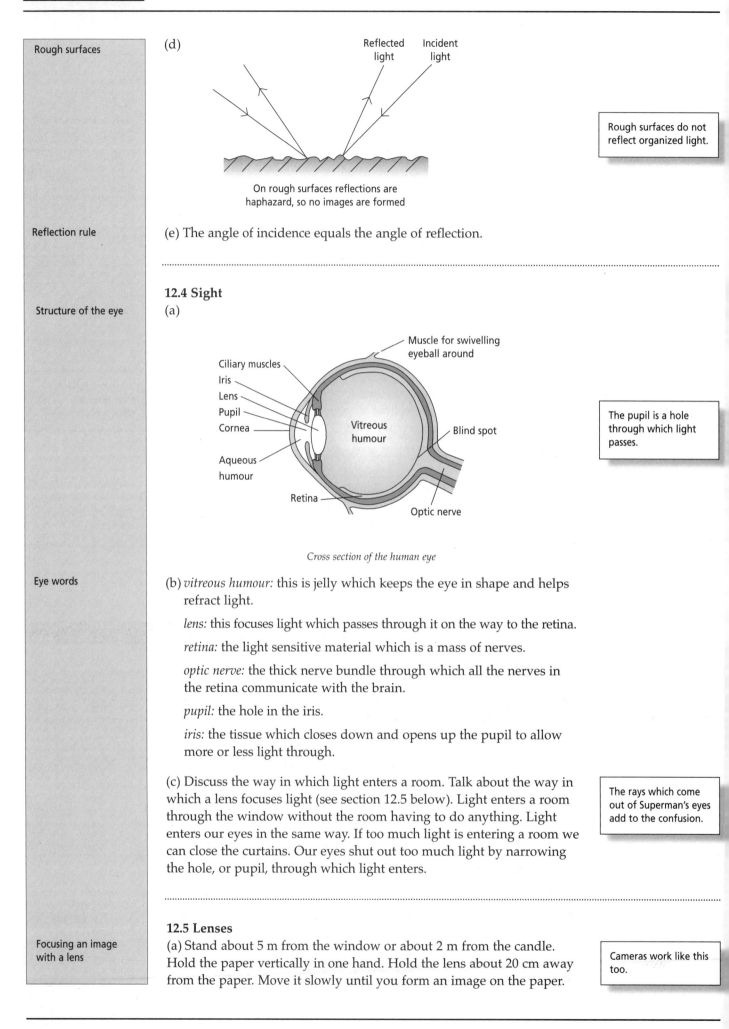

Rough surfaces

(d)

Reflected light   Incident light

On rough surfaces reflections are haphazard, so no images are formed

Rough surfaces do not reflect organized light.

Reflection rule

(e) The angle of incidence equals the angle of reflection.

Structure of the eye

12.4 Sight

(a)

Muscle for swivelling eyeball around

Ciliary muscles
Iris
Lens
Pupil
Cornea

Vitreous humour

Blind spot

Aqueous humour

Retina

Optic nerve

Cross section of the human eye

The pupil is a hole through which light passes.

Eye words

(b) *vitreous humour:* this is jelly which keeps the eye in shape and helps refract light.

lens: this focuses light which passes through it on the way to the retina.

retina: the light sensitive material which is a mass of nerves.

optic nerve: the thick nerve bundle through which all the nerves in the retina communicate with the brain.

pupil: the hole in the iris.

iris: the tissue which closes down and opens up the pupil to allow more or less light through.

(c) Discuss the way in which light enters a room. Talk about the way in which a lens focuses light (see section 12.5 below). Light enters a room through the window without the room having to do anything. Light enters our eyes in the same way. If too much light is entering a room we can close the curtains. Our eyes shut out too much light by narrowing the hole, or pupil, through which light enters.

The rays which come out of Superman's eyes add to the confusion.

12.5 Lenses

Focusing an image with a lens

(a) Stand about 5 m from the window or about 2 m from the candle. Hold the paper vertically in one hand. Hold the lens about 20 cm away from the paper. Move it slowly until you form an image on the paper.

Cameras work like this too.

(b) The image produced by the lens of our eye is upside down in exactly the same way as the image on the paper.

Key ideas summary

Light travels in **straight** lines. Where it is blocked **shadows** are formed. We see objects because light from a source is **reflected** off them into our eyes. Mirrors reflect **images** – these are reflected pictures of an object.

Visible light is just one small part of the full spectrum of **electromagnetic** radiation. Radio waves are very **long** waves and x-rays are very **short** wave radiation from this spectrum. Different coloured light has different **wavelengths**. Red has **longer** waves than blue. Infra-red radiation is heat and ultraviolet rays **tan (brown/damage)** skin in sunlight.

Red objects look red because they reflect only **red** light and absorb the other primary **colours**. When we look at white paper through a **blue** filter it appears blue because the filter absorbs the other **primary** colours and lets through blue only.

13 Sound

13.1 Vibrations and travelling sound

Sound travels through things.

(a) We know that sound can travel through the following materials:

> *air:* because we can hear things with our ears in air.

> *water:* because we can hear noises with our ears under water; whales communicate under water.

> *steel:* because we can hear tapping through steel handrails and through steel radiator pipes.

> *brick:* because we can hear the neighbours through party walls.

> *wood:* because we can hear sounds through a door.

Preventing unwanted sound in buildings is difficult.

Moon talk

(b) Astronauts communicate with each other on the moon by radio. There is a complete vacuum on the moon. Sound waves cannot travel through a vacuum but radio waves can.

Children find it difficult to imagine that sound can be converted to electricity and then converted back to sound again.

A deaf musician

(c) She plays without shoes so that she can feel the vibration of the drums and xylophones through her feet and bones.

(d) *trombone:* the air inside the tube vibrates; the longer the tube the lower the note.

organ: the air inside the pipe vibrates; the longer the pipe the lower the note.

violin: the strings vibrate; the body of the violin amplifies the vibration.

triangle: the metal vibrates.

oboe: a thin flexible reed vibrates and this makes the air inside the oboe vibrate.

13.2 Loudness and pitch

(a) *volume:* loudness; this is a measure of the energy of a sound. Loud sounds are created by vibrating objects with a large amplitude.

pitch: this is a measure of the frequency of vibration. A high-pitched sound is made by an object which vibrates very rapidly.

amplitude: the distance that a vibrating object moves. A string with a large amplitude moves a long way backwards and forwards, resulting in a loud sound.

frequency: this is the measure of the number of times the object vibrates backwards and forwards in one second. High frequency vibrations give high pitches.

(b) The tightness, length, and thickness (weight or density) of the string.

(c) The length of the tube. (The width of the tube affects the volume of the sound produced but has no bearing on its pitch.)

(d) By tightening or loosening the drum skin.

(e) If she shaves off some of the wood the pitch of the block will rise.

(f)

| Loud low pitched | Quiet low pitched | Quiet high pitched | Moderately loud moderately high pitched |

> The bass strings of a guitar are heavy to make them vibrate slowly and so have a low pitch.

> A thick drum skin has a lower pitch than a thin one.

> These are the patterns produced by oscilloscopes.

13.3 Hearing

(a) See the facing page for a labelled diagram of the human ear.

(b) *the outer ear:* the pinna gathers sound; the outer part of the eardrum is vibrated by the air.

the middle ear: hammer, anvil and stirrup bones amplify the movement of the eardrum membrane. They pass the movement to the inner ear.

> Reptiles have only one ear bone but three jaw bone parts; in mammals it is the other way round.

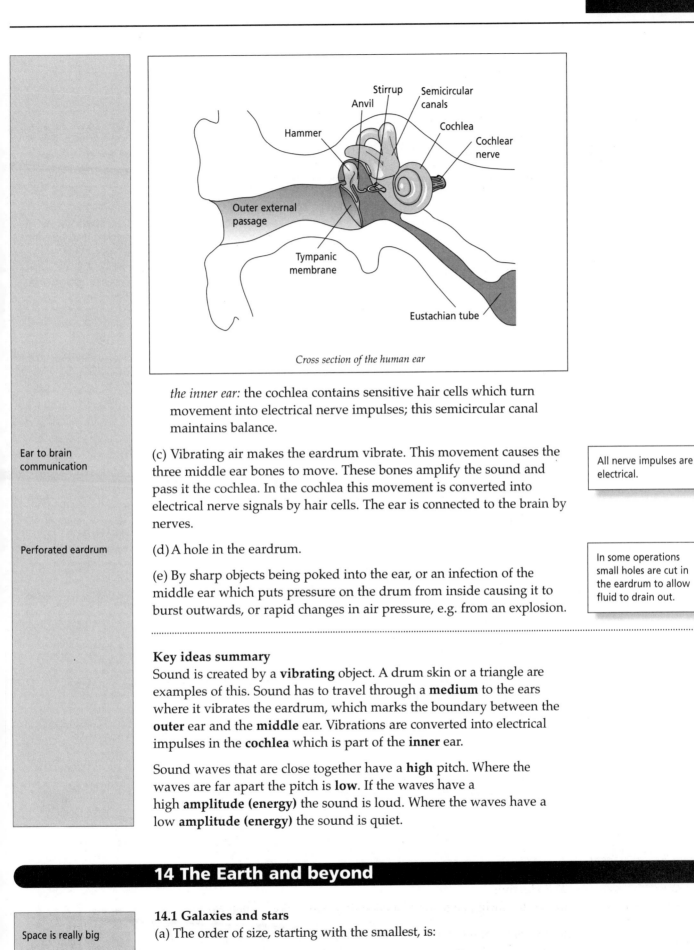

Cross section of the human ear

the inner ear: the cochlea contains sensitive hair cells which turn movement into electrical nerve impulses; this semicircular canal maintains balance.

Ear to brain communication

(c) Vibrating air makes the eardrum vibrate. This movement causes the three middle ear bones to move. These bones amplify the sound and pass it the cochlea. In the cochlea this movement is converted into electrical nerve signals by hair cells. The ear is connected to the brain by nerves.

> All nerve impulses are electrical.

Perforated eardrum

(d) A hole in the eardrum.

(e) By sharp objects being poked into the ear, or an infection of the middle ear which puts pressure on the drum from inside causing it to burst outwards, or rapid changes in air pressure, e.g. from an explosion.

> In some operations small holes are cut in the eardrum to allow fluid to drain out.

Key ideas summary

Sound is created by a **vibrating** object. A drum skin or a triangle are examples of this. Sound has to travel through a **medium** to the ears where it vibrates the eardrum, which marks the boundary between the **outer** ear and the **middle** ear. Vibrations are converted into electrical impulses in the **cochlea** which is part of the **inner** ear.

Sound waves that are close together have a **high** pitch. Where the waves are far apart the pitch is **low**. If the waves have a high **amplitude (energy)** the sound is loud. Where the waves have a low **amplitude (energy)** the sound is quiet.

14 The Earth and beyond

14.1 Galaxies and stars

Space is really big

(a) The order of size, starting with the smallest, is:

Earth: a rocky planet.
red dwarf: a collapsed star.
sun: a middle-aged, medium-sized star.

white giant star: a star which has expanded prior to collapse.
galaxy: a very large group of stars.
universe: everything / all the galaxies.

Our neighbours

(b) True. Our galaxy is called the Milky Way.

(c) False. The Andromeda galaxy is the Milky Way's nearest neighbour. It is 2.3 million light years away.

> Light takes 2.3 million years to reach us from Andromeda.

(d) False. The sun is our nearest star which is 150 million km away. Proxima Centauri is four light years away, so travelling at the speed of light you would reach it in four years.

Galaxies

(e) False. There are many types of galaxy.

The number of stars

(f) More than 100 billion stars. There are also hundreds of billions of galaxies.

> Out of all those stars it is likely that there are many Earth-like planets with life.

14.2 The solar system

The planets

(a)
1 Mercury	4 Mars	7 Uranus
2 Venus	5 Jupiter	8 Neptune
3 Earth	6 Saturn	9 Pluto

Size of planets

(b) Size, starting with the smallest:
1 Pluto	4 Venus	7 Uranus
2 Mercury	5 Earth	8 Saturn
3 Mars	6 Neptune	9 Jupiter

(c) Rocky planets

Mercury   Venus   Earth   Mars   Pluto

The others are giant gas planets.

> It is likely that particles from the sun blew away the thick gas clouds from the four inner planets soon after they were formed.

Oxygen-rich planets

(d) Earth is the only planet with an oxygen-rich atmosphere.

14.3 The moon and eclipses

(a) The sun's light is reflected off the moon's surface.

(b) One side of the moon is always lit up but we can only ever see part of this except at times when the moon is in line with the sun and the Earth, but not eclipsed.

Moon phases

(c)

Sunlight   Sunlight   Sunlight

new	crescent	half	gibbous	full	gibbous	half	crescent	new

←———— WAXING ————→   ←———— WANING ————→

New moon

Moon's orbit

Eclipses

(d) When the moon is new no part of it is visible from the Earth.

(e) About 28 days.

(f) Once. This is how it keeps the same face to the Earth all the time.

(g) New moon. This is the only point in its orbit when the moon is exactly between the Earth and the sun.

(h) The plane of the moon's orbit is at a slight angle to the plane of the Earth's orbit round the sun. If both were exactly the same there would be a solar eclipse every month.

(i) Eclipses of the moon occur when the moon is full and the shadow of the Earth blocks light from the sun. Lunar eclipses are more common than solar eclipses but they do not happen every month for the same reason that solar eclipses do not happen every month.

> Place an object on the floor. Shuffle round it facing it all the time. You face different walls as you orbit.

14.4 Day, night and seasons

Day and night

The year

Tilt of the Earth's axis

The seasons

(a) Day and night occur because the Earth turns on its axis every 24 hours.

(b) It takes the Earth just over 365 days to complete one orbit of the sun.

(c) The tilt of the Earth's axis is 23.5° from the vertical (which is why the Arctic circle and the tropics are at 23.5°).

> The tropics and the Antarctic and Arctic circles are not based on climate, they are related to the angle at which the sun shines at the Earth.

(d)

The Earth circling the sun showing summer and winter

Important lines of latitude

It is important to note that the distance from the Earth to the sun remains constant throughout the year. We do not get closer in summer.

(e) When the northern part of the planet is tilted towards the sun it is summer for that hemisphere. This is because the sun's rays are nearer to vertical so they do not spread their energy. Also, in the summer, days are longer giving more time for the sun to warm up that part of the planet.

> For a similar reason north-facing slopes are not as warm as south-facing slopes.

Solstice and equinox

(f) *equinox* is the point reached in spring and autumn when the Earth's tilt allows the sun to illuminate the north and south poles equally. All parts of the planet have equal day and night over the 24 hours of the equinox.

solstice is at midwinter and midsummer. It marks the point in the Earth's orbit when the tilt of the Earth points either the north or the south pole furthest away from the sun.

> The sun is overhead at noon twice each year at the equator.

> On the midsummer solstice the sun is overhead at noon at the Tropic of Cancer.

(g) The poles each spend six months with the sun below the horizon and six months with the sun above the horizon.

At the Arctic circle there is one night in midsummer when the sun does not set at all and one day during the winter when the sun does not rise above the horizon.

In Britain days are very short in winter but very long in summer. They even out in the course of a year.

At the equator there are approximately 12 hours of daylight each day throughout the year.

Key ideas summary
Our Earth circles the sun, which is a medium sized **star**. The solar system consists of **nine** planets circling the sun. Our star is one of billions of other **stars** in the Milky Way **galaxy**. There are hundreds of **billions** of other **galaxies**.

The **Earth** turns once a day on its axis. It takes a little over **365** days to orbit the sun. The **moon** orbits the Earth. The moon keeps one face to us which means it must complete **one** turn each month on its axis. The moon is **full** when it is on the opposite side of the Earth to the sun. The moon is **new** when it is between the sun and the Earth. **Eclipses** happen only rarely because the **moon's** orbit is tilted in relation to the Earth's orbit round the **sun**.

Further reading

The following titles have been written specifically to support the scientific knowledge and understanding needed by primary teachers in order to deliver the National Curriculum for science:

Farrow, S. (1996) *The Really Useful Science Book: A Framework of Knowledge for Primary Teachers*, London: Falmer Press.
Detailed information to support teaching of the National Curriculum programmes of study for science (Attainment Targets 2–4). Key ideas are developed into science concepts aimed specifically at Key Stages 1 and 2.

Peacock, G. and Smith, R. (1992) *Teaching and Understanding Science*, London: Hodder and Stoughton.
Scientific knowledge to help teachers develop their own understanding. Supports ATs 2–4 and suggests practical activities linked to specific scientific ideas drawn from the programmes of study.

Smith, R. and Peacock, G. (1995) *Investigations and Progression in Science*, London: Hodder and Stoughton.
Focuses on Attainment Target 1. Gives support and advice about developing children's investigative skills. Defines progression and gives detailed examples of how it can be achieved. Considers planning issues.

Wenham, M. (1995) *Understanding Primary Science: Ideas, Concepts and Explanations*, London: Paul Chapman Publishing.
Scientific facts, concepts and theories are developed with the help of practical examples and demonstrations which can be adapted for classroom use.

These are useful reference sources. Do not underestimate the ability of books written for children to demonstrate scientific ideas in a clear and accessible way:

Clugston, M. J. (1998) *The New Penguin Dictionary of Science*, Harmondsworth: Penguin Books.

Craig, A. and Rosney, C. (1997) *The Usborne Science Encyclopedia*, London: Usborne Publishing.

Stockley, C. (ed.) (1988) *The Illustrated Dictionary of Science*, London: Usborne Publishing.

Use these books to check and develop your understanding of statistics:

Cohen, L. and Holliday, P. (1996) *Practical Statistics for Students*, London: Paul Chapman Publishing.
For students with some knowledge and experience of handling statistical data.

Pentz, M. and Stott, M. (1988) *Handling Experimental Data*, Milton Keynes: Open University Press.
Basic statistics in relation to simple experimental design.

Rowntree, D. (1994) *Statistics without Tears: A Primer for Non-mathematicians*, Harmondsworth: Penguin Books.

Several dedicated web sites offer online information which can be useful to primary science teachers. These include:

Schools Online Science Project
http://www.shu.ac.uk/schools/sci/sol/contents.htm

Science Line
http://www.sciencenet.org.uk

Personal learning plan

The *Personal learning plan* is a way of planning and recording your progress as you work through this book. Choose a relatively small area of science knowledge and attempt the questions in the *Audit*. Ideally you should tackle topics which you are about to encounter on your course. Where possible work alongside a fellow student and act as study partners for each other.

Check your answers against those given in the *Feedback*. In the *Personal learning plan* briefly record in the **Initial Record of Progress** those areas you understand and know about. Draw up an **Action Plan** for those areas about which you are uncertain. Be as specific as possible about this. You may need help from your tutor or you may want to refer to some of the books and other sources of information listed in this book.

As you follow up your action points, keep a record in **Update on Progress**. For some of the more extensive areas of scientific knowledge you may need to draw up a *Personal learning plan* on a larger sheet of paper. If you are a student on an ITT course add these records to the evidence you use in support of your claim that you meet the primary science standards for the award of QTS.

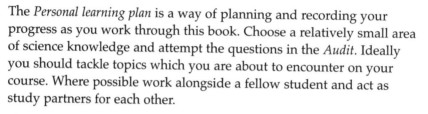

2 Scientific investigations

Initial Record of Progress	Action Plan
19 September I understand the difference between continuous and discrete data. I can draw scattergrams confidently. I understand the differences between histograms and bar charts.	Need to do more on dependent and independent variables. Need to remember which goes on which axis of the graph. Need to work on the different types of key. Will get to know the names of local trees using the key in the Collins tree book. **Update on Progress** **10 October** Used key to identify all six types of tree in the playground at school. **17 October** Worked with Jon on drawing several sketch graphs with dependent and independent variables on the correct axes.

1 The nature of science

Initial Record of Progress	Action Plan
	Update on Progress

2 Scientific investigations

Initial Record of Progress	Action Plan
	Update on Progress

3 Health and safety requirements

Initial Record of Progress	Action Plan
	Update on Progress

4 Functions of organisms

Initial Record of Progress

Action Plan

Update on Progress

5 Continuity and change

Initial Record of Progress

Action Plan

Update on Progress

6 Ecosystems and classification

Initial Record of Progress

Action Plan

Update on Progress

7 Particle theory

Initial Record of Progress

Action Plan

Update on Progress

8 Materials

Initial Record of Progress

Action Plan

Update on Progress

9 Electricity and magnetism

Initial Record of Progress

Action Plan

Update on Progress

10 Energy

Initial Record of Progress	Action Plan
	Update on Progress

11 Forces

Initial Record of Progress	Action Plan
	Update on Progress

12 Light

Initial Record of Progress

Action Plan

Update on Progress

13 Sound

Initial Record of Progress

Action Plan

Update on Progress

14 The Earth and beyond

Initial Record of Progress

Action Plan

Update on Progress